Sermon on the Mount

Sermon on the Mount:
A Beginner's Guide to the Kingdom of Heaven
978-1-5018-9989-8
978-1-5018-9990-4 eBook

Sermon on the Mount: DVD
978-1-5018-9993-5

Sermon on the Mount: Leader Guide
978-1-5018-9991-1
978-1-5018-9992-8 eBook

Also by Amy-Jill Levine

Entering the Passion of Jesus:
A Beginner's Guide to Holy Week

Light of the World:
A Beginner's Guide to Advent

AMY-JILL LEVINE

SERMON *on* *the* MOUNT

A BEGINNER'S GUIDE to the KINGDOM of HEAVEN

Abingdon Press
Nashville

SERMON ON THE MOUNT
A BEGINNER'S GUIDE TO THE KINGDOM OF HEAVEN

Library of Congress Control Number: 2020936870

ISBN-13: 978-1-5018-9989-8

Scripture quotations unless noted otherwise are from the New Revised Standard Version Bible, copyright © 1989 National Council of the Churches of Christ in the United States of America. Used by permission. All rights reserved worldwide. http://nrsvbibles.org/

Scripture quotations marked (KJV) are from The Authorized (King James) Version. Rights in the Authorized Version in the United Kingdom are vested in the Crown. Reproduced by permission of the Crown's patentee, Cambridge University Press.

Quotations from the Mishnah, including Pirke Avot, are taken from Jacob Neusner, *The Mishnah: A New Translation* (New Haven, CT: Yale University Press, 1991).

Quotations from the Babylonian Talmud are taken from the William Davidson Talmud, Sefaria.org, www.sefaria.org/texts/Talmud.

Quotations from the Dead Sea Scrolls are taken from Michael Wise, Martin Abegg Jr., and Edward Cook, *The Dead Sea Scrolls: A New Translation* (San Francisco: HarperSanFrancisco, 1996).

21 22 23 24 25 26 27 28 29—10 9 8 7 6 5 4 3
MANUFACTURED IN THE UNITED STATES OF AMERICA

Dedicated with special gratitude to The Temple (Congregation Ohabai Shalom) in Nashville, Tennessee, which has for two decades welcomed not only Jews but also Christians and the religiously unaffiliated to study with me, for three weeks a year, texts and histories that Jews and Christians share, including the Sermon on the Mount. Those nights at The Temple are evidence of the kingdom of heaven in our midst.

CONTENTS

INTRODUCTION

Who Wants to Read a Sermon?

When I first read the Gospel of Matthew—I must have been about thirteen or fourteen—I didn't have much interest in the Sermon on the Mount. The Christmas story with the magi and the slaughter of the innocents, the Baptism, Jesus's calling his first four disciples, the Temptation (loved the Temptation! Jesus 3, Satan 0)—all these action-filled, character-driven passages—these fascinated me. And then Matthew 5–7, the Sermon. The Bible I had titled these three chapters "The Sermon on the Mount," and the very word *sermon* stopped me. I didn't want to read a sermon. Given the number of sermons I had heard in my "junior congregation" services at my hometown synagogue, I was pretty sure that "sermon" was synonymous with "boring" or "obvious." In the local Catholic church that I attended with friends, I had heard a few homilies (for a while I thought the term was *hominies*, like grits). The only thing that made homilies better than sermons was that they tended to be shorter.

Who wants to read a sermon, even if it is by Jesus? I skipped over Matthew 5–7 fairly quickly and then got to the good parts where Jesus starts healing people and arguing with other Jews.

When I got to college and took Introduction to the New Testament—I was eighteen—I still didn't have much interest in the Sermon on the Mount. The reasons for this lack of interest, however, had changed. When I mentioned to my Christian friends, whether in high school or in my first year of college, that I was interested in biblical studies and especially in the New Testament, many of these friends sang the same song: "Oh yes," they said, "we learned a lot about Jesus in church. We learned that he came to fix Judaism, which had gone downhill from the good old days of Abraham. Problems started with Moses and the Law, and then they got increasingly worse. The Jewish system was legalistic, misogynistic, xenophobic, violent, lacking in mercy, and otherwise a mess." That's why, they told me, Jesus gave the Sermon on the Mount, with its comments about "You have heard it said . . . but I say to you . . .": to replace the Torah's "eye for an eye" with Jesus's "turn the other cheek." That's why, they told me, Jesus had to teach his followers how to pray, because the Jews had forgotten.

Who wants to read a sermon if the whole point is to show that Judaism had devolved into something disgusting? Rather than read the text for myself, I simply took their word for it and, again, went from the Temptation in Matthew 4 to the healing of the man with leprosy in Matthew 8 (free health care—what's not to like?).

Alas, I didn't know what I was missing because I stuck with what I had been told rather than what I had learned for myself. This concern has become a guide for me now as a professor. I ask my students to think about two questions when they write their papers and sermons. The first question is, How do I know this? They need to back up their claims rather than go with what they've always been told since their preschool days, settle for the easy answer, or retroject twenty-first-century sensibilities onto first-century texts. The second question is, Why do I care? If they can show their own interest and show how they've been inspired by the text, they are better able to convey the good news to others.

Then, about midway through my first year at Smith College, I had an aha moment, in great measure thanks to my New Testament professor, Karl Donfried. Professor Donfried knew the history, and he knew why the text mattered. He helped me see that Jesus is not a Christian talking to other Christians; he is a Jew talking to other Jews. He's not telling his fellow Jews to do away with Torah. That would be ridiculous. Rather, he's telling them that he has insight into the heart of Torah, and they would do well to listen to him. I started to read the Sermon on the Mount as a teaching given by one Jew to fellow Jews.

Finally, everything clicked. The Sermon on the Mount is not a sermon. It's a series of discrete teachings, each of which could be the basis of a sermon, a lecture, a community study, or a personal meditation. Had Jesus delivered all verses in Matthew 5–7 at one time, the disciples' heads would have exploded. There's too much in these chapters to absorb in a single lesson. Every verse is a multifaceted gem, and every line opens up to other passages in the Gospel. (You can probably sense my frustration: there's so much more to say than the six chapters in this study can contain.)

When I read Matthew 5–7, I found neither a sermon nor a boring text; I found that neither sermons nor lectures nor studies need be boring. As I tell my students, "When you prepare to give a sermon, study what others have said and then determine what you need to say to your own congregation. If you put in the work, the sermon should be stirring and inspirational rather than boring and banal." With Jesus as our teacher for the Sermon on the Mount, we are guaranteed to be engaged.

The problem is marketing: the Sermon on the Mount could easily be retitled "A Sampling of Jesus's Greatest Teachings." That would not be uncommon for literature in antiquity. The rabbinic document *Pirke Avot* (*Ethics of the Fathers*), to which we shall return in this study, is in effect the "Rabbis' Greatest Hits." Here's where we find such gems as "On three things does the world stand: On the Torah, and on the Temple service, and on deeds of loving kindness" (Avot 1:2) and "On three things does the world stand: on justice, on truth, and on peace" (Avot 1:18). They don't agree, and they are both right. We'll find that in many cases, the teachings of the rabbis and of Jesus complement each other.

The problem is the label "Sermon on the Mount," a label Matthew never uses. These three chapters tell us that the kingdom of heaven is not some abstract place with pearly gates and golden slippers, harp music, and a bunch of angels flapping their wings. The kingdom of heaven occurs when people take the words of Jesus in these chapters to heart and live into them. In this book, we begin with the Beatitudes, move to Jesus's Torah interpretation, see what Jesus says about practicing piety (a great section for those—of course, no one reading *this* study—whose practice of faith is more of a "look at me" than a "look to God"), encounter the Our Father prayer, and see how profound it is when heard through the ears of a first-century Jew living in the Roman Empire. We then move to Jesus's wise words about how we find our treasures, and how easily we are distracted by what we don't actually need. We end with "Living into the Kingdom": now that we have been blessed and challenged, inspired and chided, comforted and made uncomfortable, we realize what this is: the Sermon on the Mount is in fact a beginner's guide to the kingdom of heaven.

The Kingdom of Heaven—Taking the First Steps

The terms "kingdom of heaven" and "kingdom of God" can be synonymous, but they have different nuances. For example, in some places where Mark uses the expression "Kingdom of God," Matthew has "Kingdom of heaven." In Mark 1:15, Jesus proclaims, "The time is fulfilled, and the *kingdom of God* has come near; repent, and believe in the good news" (italics added). Matthew likely used the Gospel of Mark as a source, and in Matthew 3:2, we see a bit of Matthew's editing. Here, the Baptist says, "Repent, for the *kingdom of heaven* has come near" (italics added). In Luke's Gospel and in John's, Jesus always speaks of the "kingdom of God" and *never* uses the expression "kingdom of heaven."

The argument has been made that Matthew uses "kingdom of heaven" instead of "kingdom of God" because, as a Jew, Matthew would not use the name of God in vain and so used "heaven" as a circumlocution (a way to say God without saying God, as we might say today, "Good heavens" rather than "Good God"). However, that cannot be the case, for Matthew also uses the expression "kingdom of God." As Jesus instructs his disciples in the Sermon on the Mount, "But strive first for the kingdom of God and his righteousness, and all these things will be given to you as well" (6:33).

Since Matthew also uses "kingdom of God" as well as the word *God* about fifty times, *heaven* cannot be a stand-in for *God*. Rather, Matthew is setting up a contrast between heaven and earth: heaven is where God's will is done; heaven is where God rules rather than where the "kings of the earth" who "take toll or tribute" (17:25) hold sway. Heaven is a different place, a better place, a real place, a place where God rules and life is as God wants rather than as humanity has constructed. Consequently, Jesus instructs his disciples to pray "Your kingdom come" (6:10) because on earth, the rule of the divine is not fully manifest (more on this when we get to the Our Father prayer in chapter 4).

This kingdom of heaven, where God rules, is both present (since God our father is in heaven) and future, since that divine reign is still not fully present on earth. As both John the Baptist and Jesus state, "Repent, for the kingdom of heaven has come near" (3:2; 4:17). When we "repent"—which is not simply a matter of saying we are sorry for doing the sinful thing or failing to do the right thing but is also a matter of fixing what we have done wrong, of getting off the wrong path and onto the right one—that kingdom has come near. But it will be even more glorious, for as Jesus teaches, "many will come from east and west and will eat with Abraham and Isaac and Jacob in the kingdom of heaven" (8:11). That kingdom of heaven is a place and a time when past, present, and future unite, when we recline at table with our ancestors, and when borders are open to the east and west so that Jews and Gentiles worship God together.

The Sermon on the Mount, as we shall see through the next six chapters, is the beginner's guide to the kingdom of heaven. But we should not stop at a beginner's guide any more than we should stop at Matthew 7, the end of the Sermon. When Jesus states toward the end of the Sermon, "In everything do to others as you would have them do to you; for this is the law and the prophets" (7:12)—what we today call the Golden Rule—he is not saying that *all* we need to do is based on our own needs and desires. I have heard far too often the claim that if we know the Golden Rule, we know Jesus. Were this the case, then we could toss the rest of the Gospel, or the rest of the New Testament, into the Sea of Galilee. Jesus is rather providing a guideline for assessing our actions. The Sermon on the Mount, placed so early in the New Testament, should be the template through which we read the rest of the text.

We also do well to read Matthew 7:12, the Golden Rule, alongside a story about the famous Rabbi Hillel, Jesus's slightly older contemporary. As the story goes, a potential convert approaches Hillel and demands, "Convert me on condition that you teach me the entire Torah while I am standing on one foot." Hillel responds, "That which is hateful to you do not do to another; that is the entire Torah, and the rest is its interpretation. Go study" (Babylonian Talmud Shabbat 31a).

Matthew would say the same: if you want to understand the kingdom of heaven, do not limit yourself to the Golden Rule or the Sermon on the Mount. Instead, realize that the entire Gospel is part of the guide. Matthew is a brilliant writer: chapters 1–4 anticipate the Sermon; chapters 8–28 provide echoes of it, and when we read the Gospel a second, third, fourth, and fourteen-thousandth time, we will continue to pick up new echoes. When we read the rest of the New Testament in light of Matthew 5–7, we will hear echoes continually, in Paul's letters, in the Epistle of James, even in Revelation.

Matthew's Narrative Genius

The first four chapters in Matthew's Gospel are a beginner's guide to Jesus: where he came from, who he is, how he fulfills prophecy, how he relates to righteousness, how he submits to John the Baptist, how he fights with the devil. The words and actions—not only of Jesus but also of the women in the genealogy, of Joseph, and of John the Baptist—in these opening chapters create a first link, a lovely prelude to the Sermon. Here are four of the many instances where we see the themes of the Sermon anticipated (and should you read Matthew 5–7 and then go back and read the first four chapters, your eyes—those lamps of the body, as the Sermon puts it—will necessarily be opened to new insights).

Tamar, Rahab, Ruth, and Bathsheba, the first four women mentioned in the New Testament, display a *higher righteousness* by acting in surprising ways in order to advance Israel's history. Judah, Tamar's father-in-law by whom she conceives twins (another story for another time), even states that she is "more *righteous* than I" (Genesis 38:26 KJV). Joseph, whom Matthew identifies as *"righteous"* (1:19), accepts the angel's command to marry Mary, pregnant but not with his child; more, he protects both mother and child by taking them to Egypt and then relocating from Bethlehem to Nazareth. (There's an old Yiddish curse: "You should have to move twice in a year.")

Thus, when Jesus states in the Sermon, "Blessed are those who hunger and thirst *for righteousness*, for they will be filled" (5:6), we should immediately think of Tamar, left as a levirate widow and trapped by her father-in-law, Judah, from marrying again. We should think of Rahab, who protects not only the Israelites who enter her city of Jericho but also strikes a deal with them so that she can protect her own family. We are reminded of the widowed Moabite Ruth, who becomes a stranger in a strange land when she, together with her mother-in-law, Naomi, enters Bethlehem and begins to glean in Boaz's field. We are reminded not only of Bathsheba but also of her first husband, Uriah the Hittite, the faithful foreign soldier who refused to violate Israel's rules of holy war. And before we're finished with chapter 1, we find another model of righteousness: Joseph, who "being a righteous man" (1:19) resolved to divorce his pregnant fiancée, Mary, without making a spectacle of

Introduction

her. In chapter 3, John the Baptist tells Jesus, whom he recognizes as the Messiah, "You should baptize me" (v. 14). But Jesus insists that John perform the rite, for "it is proper for us in this way to fulfill all righteousness" (v. 15).

When Jesus states, "Blessed are those who are persecuted for righteousness' sake, for theirs is the kingdom of heaven" (5:10), we are reminded of the genealogy's mention of the deportation of the population to Babylon (today we would call this forced migration), of Mary, Joseph, and Jesus, forced to flee to Egypt to escape political persecution by Herod (today we would call them asylum seekers). We are again reminded of John the Baptist, who will be executed by Herod Antipas (see Matthew 14) for condemning his marriage to his sister-in-law Herodias and thereby violating the commandment against what ancient Israel saw as incest.

The temptation narrative in Matthew 4, the first encounter between Jesus and the devil, provides a second link to the Sermon on the Mount. Jesus asks nothing of us that he does not do himself. The fully human Jesus, through his own strong faith and grounding in his tradition, provides the guide for living. When he instructs his disciples to pray "lead us not into temptation"—better translated as "do not bring us to the test"—we already know what to do in case that test comes. Jesus himself was tempted, or tested, by Satan, and he passed the test by relying on the Word of God, by citing as well as enacting the Book of Deuteronomy. How do we overcome temptation and keep ourselves on the path to the kingdom? We use the resources God has already given us: Scripture, what Christians have come to call the Old Testament. We return to this testing when we look at the Lord's Prayer in chapter 4.

A third connection surfaces in Jesus's comment, "Do not think that I have come to abolish the law or the prophets; I have come not to abolish but to fulfill" (5:17). Those first four chapters (and not just the infancy narratives) not only show Jesus to fulfill prophecy but also establish Jesus as the "New Moses," the one who comes not to abolish Torah but to interpret it. Jesus is not only "son of

Abraham," "son of David," and "Son of God" but also for his followers the fulfillment of Deuteronomy 18:18, where God says, "I will raise up for them a prophet like you [Moses] from among their own people; I will put my words in the mouth of the prophet, who shall speak to them everything that I command."

It is no accident that the Sermon on the Mount is *on the mountain*, for that mountain should remind us of Mount Sinai, where Moses delivered the Torah to Israel. Matthew sets another six scenes on mountains: in the temptation narrative, the devil took Jesus to "a very high mountain and showed him all the kingdoms of the world and their splendor" (4:8).

In 14:23, Jesus ascends a mountain to pray, and in 15:29-38, from a mountain, Jesus feeds the five thousand (we should be reminded of the manna in the wilderness). It will be on a mountain in Matthew 17 that Jesus appears with Moses and Elijah (representing the Torah and the Prophets, and also representing individuals who encountered God on a mountaintop) and where Jesus is transfigured (the Greek term is *metamorphosis*). On a mountain (Matthew 24:3), Jesus describes to his disciples what will happen when the kingdom of heaven triumphs over the kingdoms of the earth. And on a mountain, Jesus issues the Great Commission to his disciples (28:16-20).

The Sermon on the Mount (and Matthew's concern for mountains) is a distinguishing characteristic of the First Gospel. Parallel material appears in Luke 6:12-20, traditionally called the Sermon on the Plain. (I can't tell you how many students identify this section as the "Sermon on the Plane," as if Jesus is giving directions on what to do in case of turbulence.) Each sermon has much to offer, and each is better appreciated when seen as part of its own Gospel.

Matthew's first four chapters prepare us for the Sermon; the rest of the Gospel becomes the Sermon in action. Our response to the stories—and not merely an intellectual assent or an aesthetic pleasure but our response in action—is the gateway to the kingdom of heaven. Once we walk through this gate, we are better listeners and so better recipients of the parables told to the disciples "to know the secrets of the kingdom of heaven" (13:11). We are better prepared when Jesus instructs, "Unless you change and become like children, you will never enter the kingdom of heaven" (18:3). The point is not to behave in a childish manner. Jesus is speaking about an attitude of trust, a recognition that we are dependent on others, a recollection that we are part of the family of God. When we adopt this attitude, we can live into the Sermon when it tells us not to worry (and more on this topic in chapter 5).

Reading the Sermon Without Despairing

For Martin Luther, the Sermon on the Mount offered an impossible ideal, for we can never love our enemies or be perfect. Luther spoke of a "counsel of despair"—a list of instructions that no one could follow—and I can see where he would get this idea. Verses such as "Love your enemies and pray for those who persecute you" (5:44) or "Be perfect, therefore, as your heavenly Father is perfect" (5:48) can be off-putting. I have no immediate interest in loving my enemy; hate is so much easier. I can't be perfect, nor do I want to be. But Jesus is not demanding of us what we are incapable of doing.

Jesus is not telling us, in these chapters, how horrible we are. To the contrary, the Sermon on the Mount assures us that we are wondrous creatures with unlimited potential. We already have the gifts needed to live into the kingdom of heaven. Jewish tradition does not in general dwell on how broken we are, how sinful, how fallen. It teaches that all human beings are in the image and likeness of the divine. That means we must see that divine image in the face of everyone—not just the cute baby, not just the radiant bride, not just the elderly gabbai in the synagogue who always greets us at the door. We have to see the image of the divine in those it would be so easy to hate: the Nazis who are among us to this day, the terrorists who seek to die a martyr's death by blowing up themselves and all around them, the child molester. They, too, are human beings.

Hate takes up too much energy; loving is in fact easier. Combatting those who espouse bigotry today is much harder, but hating them is not a productive step.

The Sermon on the Mount is not a counsel of despair; it is a hymn of praise not only to God but also for all creation. Jesus tells his disciples, "You are the light of the world" (5:14). Otherwise put, we are fabulous creatures. In John 9:5, Jesus states, "As long as I am in the world, I am the light of the world." When he is no longer physically present, he is represented by his disciples. Thus the Sermon on the Mount resembles, in part, a theological pep talk. Good pep talks, or revivals, don't just make us feel better about ourselves. They inspire us not just to feel better but to do better: try harder, dig more deeply, find the resources needed for living the life to which God is calling us. Let that light shine so that others can see, even amid your struggles, that you have spiritual resources, and the covenant community, to persevere.

Hearing Old Songs in a New Key

We've already noted how the Sermon reminds us of Moses. That connection is only the start of a much deeper motif, for the Sermon frequently references the Scriptures of Israel. If we miss the connections, we'll miss just how extraordinarily rich these three Gospel chapters are.

For example, the Beatitudes ("blessed are . . ."), to which we turn in chapter 1, are a form of blessings found throughout Israel's Scriptures and rabbinic literature (writings of the ancient Jewish sages, including the Mishnah and the Talmud). It would not be weird to suggest that people who are in need—of comfort, of righteousness, of peace—are blessed. Isaiah 30:18 already proclaimed,

> Therefore the LORD waits to be gracious to you;
> therefore he will rise up to show mercy to you.

For the Lord is a God of justice;
  blessed are all those who wait for him.

Jeremiah 17:7 reads, "Blessed are those who trust in the Lord, / whose trust is the Lord."

When Jesus says, "Blessed are those who mourn, for they will be comforted" (5:4), I cannot but think of Matthew 2, the account of the murder of Bethlehem's children by Herod's soldiers, and the evangelist's note,

"A voice was heard in Ramah,
  wailing and loud lamentation,
Rachel weeping for her children;
  she refused to be consoled, because they are no more." (v. 18)

The citation is to Jeremiah 31:15, but the very next verse in Jeremiah is God's comforting Rachel and telling her that her children will return. When Matthew tells us that Jesus's followers will mourn when he is taken away from them (9:15), we already know that the period of mourning will end because of the Resurrection. But that is not all "blessed are those who mourn" means.

Regarding the so-called antitheses, the passages that begin, "You have heard it said . . . but I say to you . . ."—the title is wrong. They are not antitheses but extensions, interpretations of the Torah. Jesus interprets Torah—of course! That's what Jews do; we interpret Torah. We don't always agree with each other on the meaning of the text or how a particular mitzvah (Hebrew for "commandment" but with the connotation of "good deed" or "the right thing to do") should be carried out, but we know at the end of the day, no matter how much we disagree, we're all still Jews. And we also know that while today we may hold fast to a particular interpretation, it is always possible that tomorrow we may conclude that our neighbor is right. Hence, rabbinic literature typically preserves two or three or even more interpretations of the same text. More on this in chapter 2.

The Sermon gives detailed instructions on how to practice

piety, since Jesus, like his Jewish tradition, is concerned not only with what people believe but also, especially, with what we do. Almsgiving, fasting, and praying are not just good ideas to be considered; they are for Jesus and for his fellow Jews commandments to be followed. But, like all commandments, there are better ways and less good ways of acting. Jesus, who is particularly concerned with hypocrisy—wherein our hearts and our heads are not operating in harmony—provides instruction, some of it perhaps counterintuitive, to how we fast and pray and provide. This is our topic for chapter 3.

Chapter 4 introduces the famous Our Father prayer, sometimes called the Lord's Prayer, a perfectly good Jewish prayer. The prayer is neither innovative nor controversial; it is rather a beautiful epitome of other prayers Jews have said before and since. But it only reveals its full implications if we understand how the term *Father* was used, how one is to "hallow" the divine name, why "lead us not into temptation" is better translated "do not bring us to the test," what "daily bread" means in its first-century Jewish context, and what deliverance from evil has to do with biblical knowledge. And so we turn to chapter 4.

In chapter 5, we address the always fraught question of Jesus and economics: from his counsel on not storing up treasures on earth, to his insistence on giving to those who beg, to his warnings that we cannot serve God and mammon (the Aramaic term for "wealth," or more broadly, "stuff"). He is not, as we will see, making impossible demands or even overly idealistic ones. Once we see how he expects those who are gathered in his name to function, and once we can truly depend on others in our community—which is, as we will see, a new family—then his comments on economics make abundant sense, for they show us how we can find our treasure.

We will also see in chapter 5 how to find our treasure in the natural world, for it is in the Sermon on the Mount where Jesus instructs that we pay attention to the world around us, the birds and the lilies, the trees and the rivers. We can't pay attention to the birds if they stop singing and we have a silent spring; we can't pay attention to the lilies if they are replaced by parking lots. When Jesus speaks of God caring for the ravens, then we—who are in the image of God—should do so as well. Here we already can hear echoes of the earlier scripture where nature testifies to the glory of God—such as the creation of the natural world in Genesis 1, Psalm 104 with its praise to God for creating that world, and Psalm 19, where the natural world returns its praise to God: "The heavens are telling the glory of God; / and the firmament proclaims his handiwork" (v. 1).

In chapter 6, we see how we live into the kingdom in terms of appropriate expenditure of resources, prioritizing our actions, entering by the narrow gate, and especially how we follow the Golden Rule without imposing our own concerns on others. The gate may be narrow, but we are assured, "knock, the door will be opened for you" (Matthew 7:7). The disciples, in their early enthusiasm, might have thought that going on a mission would be the proverbial piece of cake. What is opened to us is not the easy road or the comfy living room; it is the world of need, of hurt, of loneliness, and it is this world where the lilies and the ravens, and all God's creatures, are loved and need love.

Once we get our priorities straight, then continuing to study the Sermon on the Mount helps us come to a better knowledge of ourselves. The point is not that Jesus is an ancient version of Dear Abby or Sigmund Freud (both Jewish, by the way). Rather, the Sermon—like the parables—surfaces good questions about where our values should be located and how to secure them upon a firm foundation. Indeed, throughout much of the Sermon on the Mount, Jesus is actually talking about prioritizing: What's important, and what's less important? What do we want to be known for directly, and what has us scattered? What pulls us in different directions, and how better do we focus?

Getting on the Path

All Gospels have signature stories. Each Gospel takes its interpretive key from the signature scene. For Matthew, the signature is the Sermon on the Mount. For Luke, it's the synagogue sermon in chapter 4. For Mark, it's the double healing of the blind man in chapter 8, which precedes Peter's confession. For John, it's the prologue, "In the beginning was the Word." The Sermon on the Mount, with its presentation of Jesus as a new Moses who interprets Torah, who offers wisdom sayings on how to live the way God wants, who provides practical instruction, deserves to be savored. It also deserves to be read closely, lest we wind up thinking, as do a few in the crowd according to Monty Python's *Life of Brian*, that Jesus spoke of "cheesemakers" rather than "peacemakers."

As we read through Matthew 5–7 together, we'll see how understanding Jesus's Jewish context, and Jewish message, helps us make more sense of his teaching. We can, knowing this context, get a better sense of how his teachings would have resonated with his first followers, even as we see how this very Jewish message could have easily been exported to the Gentile (that is, pagan) world. As always, we do not need to make Judaism look bad in order to make Jesus look good. And if we know the context, we can see that Jesus is even wiser, more profound, than we might have imagined.

The Sermon on the Mount tells us what we need to do in order to have one foot in the kingdom of heaven. More than that, it tells us that this kingdom is already available to us, already manifested when we enact God's will on earth as it is done in heaven. What Jesus does in a splendid way is model how we see the kingdom when we may not have realized it has been there, beckoning to us all along.

Jesus sets the model. And now that the model is set, he says to his disciples, "OK, let me show you how to do it. Here's your beginner's guide to walking as if you live in the kingdom of heaven. Here's your beginner's guide to seeing that if you just open your eyes and use your hearts, you will find that you are already there."

Chapter 1

THE BEATITUDES

Preparing for Discipleship

Jesus ascends a mountain and sits down. He does not sit down, contrary to the claims of numerous Christian interpreters, because rabbis taught while seated. Rabbis taught on any occasion and from any position they could. He sits because he's about to talk for three chapters; his disciples then come and sit near him.

Matthew 5:1 tells us that the Sermon is not delivered to outsiders; it's delivered to four disciples, insiders who have already left their homes and their families in order to follow this Galilean charismatic healer and teacher. We know from Matthew 10 that there are (at least) twelve disciples, but to this point, we've only seen him call four: Peter and Andrew, James and John. Since Matthew does not name the disciples who join Jesus on the mountain, any of us can find ourselves among those sitting close and listening.

But if we count ourselves among the disciples, our task is not simply to absorb. We are human beings, not sponges. We know from both Jewish and pagan sources that disciples are active learners: they ask questions, they seek clarification, they raise objections, they seek to take their teacher's comments to the next level. Were my students only to parrot what I said, without developing their own views, then I would have failed as a teacher. Our job, as listeners, is to study the Sermon, ask our own questions, and then, in community, seek our own answers. In churches, the congregation ideally listens to the sermon, but in few congregations is there a "talk back," let alone a challenge. In my synagogue, on a rare occasion, a member of the congregation will actually challenge the rabbi, not from a position of disrespect. Rather, the concern is full understanding, full support for an argument, clarity. That is active listening.

As a teacher, I can imagine Jesus thinking as he begins the Sermon what I think as I begin a class: *Please, folks, pay attention; don't screw this up. If you don't understand something, ask. My reputation is on the line.*

Sometimes teachers don't know the impact they have had on students. As I was putting my notes together for this chapter, I found myself as a guest speaker at a tall-steeple (that is, traditionally large and influential) Methodist church where a former PhD student of mine was head pastor. Driving from the airport to the hotel, she said to me, "You know, for a while I really hated you." Her eyes were on the road; mine were fixed on her. Not knowing what to say, I figured I'd let her talk. Then she said, as she still concentrated on the road, "You pushed me." Then she smiled.

It was true. Her "good" was already "great": she could preach the roof off the church; she could find nuances in the text that escaped the most brilliant of exegetes. But I had the impression she could do so much more, so I showed her how. Along with the A on the paper, there was also a swath of red markings with my questions: What about this? Have you considered that? How might the nuance of the Greek change the reading? Did you read the latest article on your topic? I take my pedagogical cue from Jesus: he's working already with disciples who have climbed the mountain. Now he wants them to take the next steps. Your "good" could always be better. You may be the salt of the earth, you may be the light of the world, but your salt could be saltier and your light could be brighter. Follow him into the Sermon, down the mountain, and out into the world, and step into the kingdom of heaven.

On the simple level, to go up the mountain is to risk one's balance: our ears might pop; we might get dizzy; we might trip. Or we might hear something we cannot handle. Making the climb is the first step, and it is already a commitment. Staying on the summit and realizing we could do even more requires more courage, and letting that experience transform us, transfigure us, is scarier still. But the effort is worthwhile. The vista is gorgeous. And we become cities set on a hill—but we're not there yet.

We disciples are not the only ones listening. Jesus sees the crowds, and he likely knows they will be listening in. The message is explicitly for his disciples, but they are not the only ones welcome to receive it. The crowd needs to hear the message as well, lest they misunderstand Jesus. They have been following him for a chapter, since as Matthew tells us, his fame had spread throughout Syria (4:24). But they are following him not because of his teachings but because of his health care: the crowds are coming with the afflicted, the possessed, the disabled, and they are seeking a cure. For the Gospel writers, Jesus gives sight to the blind and the ability to walk to those who cannot, but his primary role is not that of mobile medical center. His primary role is not that of miracle worker or exorcist. Not all, then or now, receive healing of the body. To the contrary, by speaking to those who are in mourning, as we shall see, Jesus recognizes that frailty of the human form.

Jesus's import is not that he works miracles. Others do miracles: Elijah and Elisha from the Scriptures of Israel, the Rabbis Honi the Circle-Drawer and Haninah ben Dosa from postbiblical Jewish texts, even Peter and Paul, according to the Book of Acts. More important than his miracles are, for the Gospels, Jesus's death and resurrection and his teachings. A healing is very good news for the individual so blessed, but even the able bodied can find ourselves in the Beatitudes, for we may all find ourselves mourning or meek, poor in spirit, or peacemakers.

Jesus begins with a series of nine statements traditionally called beatitudes, from the Latin term for "blessed." Luke's parallel has only four of these beatitudes, each balanced by a woe. Thus for Luke, "Blessed are you who are poor" (Luke 6:20) is matched by "woe to you who are rich" (Luke 6:24). No woes, at least not yet, in Matthew's version. The Sermon starts with what is entirely good news. In a few cases where Matthew and Luke give different versions of the same beatitude, we'll discuss the implications of the changes. Our concern is not that one got it right and one wrong or that Matthew and Luke are working at cross-purposes. Rather, each *evangelist* (the technical term for a Gospel author; literally, a "good-news giver") has a particular understanding of the message of Jesus.

The Beatitudes have a cultural familiarity, even to people who have not heard them read in churches: "Blessed are the poor in spirit, for theirs is the kingdom of heaven" (Matthew 5:3), "Blessed are the meek, for they will inherit the earth" (5:5), and so on. They are so familiar that some Christian theologians see them as Jesus's own autobiography: he is poor in spirit; he mourns (for example, over Jerusalem); he hungers and thirsts for righteousness. We can read the Beatitudes as Jesus's summary of his autobiography; I think we need to do more. The disciples did not initially understand Jesus to be talking about himself; they understood him to be talking about the human condition. Jesus does not need to bless himself, but people who are lost and least, mourning and meek, need to be assured that they are blessed. Theology and ethics need not be mutually exclusive.

Problems arise when we do not consider what *blessed* connotes, who the poor in spirit are, or what *meek* would have meant to Matthew's first audience. Here's how we'll proceed: we'll talk about what a beatitude is supposed to do, and then we'll look closely at several of the beatitudes to see what they would have sounded like to the Jewish ears that first heard them, to hear their echoes of Israel's Scriptures, and to realize how they still speak necessary messages to the twenty-first century. Our concern, as always, is not to strip out Christian theology but to enhance it by providing the historical context of Jesus and his followers. Fully to understand Jesus requires some understanding of what his words would have meant to the people who first heard them.

What Is a Beatitude?

Simply put, a beatitude is a blessing. The Greek term translated in most English Bibles as "blessed" is *makarioi*; hence, sometimes the beatitudes are called *makarisms*. (In an Introduction to the New Testament course at Vanderbilt a few years ago, one student told me she remembered the term because it reminded her of macaroons, also a blessing.) Preparing the Latin translation of the New Testament in the late fourth century, St. Jerome translated the Greek with *beati*, which has the connotation not only of "blessed" but also of "happy" and even "rich."

Jesus's native language was neither Latin nor Greek but Aramaic and, possibly, some Hebrew. It is not clear what the original word would have been. One possibility is the Hebrew *baruch*, which means "blessed." That is the term that begins most Jewish prayers to this day: "Blessed are you, Lord our God." We can see a similar formulation to the Beatitudes in ecologically friendly Jeremiah 17:7-8,

> Blessed are those who trust in the LORD,
> whose trust is the LORD.
> They shall be like a tree planted by water,
> sending out its roots by the stream.
> It shall not fear when heat comes,
> and its leaves shall stay green;
> in the year of drought it is not anxious,
> and it does not cease to bear fruit.

Perhaps more familiar is Psalm 118:26, "Blessed is the one who comes in the name of the LORD" (quoted in regard to Jesus in Matthew 21:9, 23:39; Mark 11:9; Luke 13:35).

Another possibility is that behind the Greek is the Hebrew word *ashrei*, which means "happy," "fortunate," or "worthy of praise." This expression appears in Isaiah 30:18,

> Therefore the LORD waits to be gracious to you;
>> therefore he will rise up to show mercy to you.
> For the LORD is a God of justice;
>> Happy [*ashrei*] are all those who wait for him.

The New Revised Standard Version actually translates that last line not as "happy are" but as "blessed are." Neatly, the Septuagint (the Greek translation of the Hebrew Bible) for Isaiah 30:18 reads for the Hebrew *ashrei* the Greek *makarioi*, the same term used in the Beatitudes.

We might also think of Psalm 84, which has resonances with the Sermon on the Mount. The first four verses of the Psalm read:

> How lovely is your dwelling place,
>> O LORD of hosts!
> My soul longs, indeed it faints
>> for the courts of the LORD;
> my heart and my flesh sing for joy
>> to the living God.

> Even the sparrow finds a home,
>> and the swallow a nest for herself,
>> where she may lay her young,
> at your altars, O LORD of hosts,
>> my King and my God.
> Happy [Hebrew: *ashrei*; Greek: *makarioi*] are those who live
> in your house,
>> ever singing your praise. Selah

Jews traditionally recite three times a day a prayer called the Ashrei, from its first word. The prayer begins, "Happy [*ashrei*] are those who live in your house, ever singing your praise, Selah!" The prayer is mostly Psalm 145, but the opening line comes from Psalm 84:4—in modern musical terms, we'd call this ancient prayer a mash-up. By the way, I looked up the term *ashrei* on the internet to be sure of getting a coherent transliteration (that is, putting the Hebrew letters into English), but I think I must have misspelled the term because the first hit I got was to the American Society of Heating, Refrigerating, and Air-Conditioning Engineers, abbreviated ASHRAE. They're blessed too.

We read the Beatitudes as indicating "Blessed are," "Happy are," "Fortunate are," "Praiseworthy are." I've also heard the translation "Congratulations," which sounded to me like the exclamation "Mazel tov" (Hebrew for "good luck" with the connotation of the Australian "Good on you"). I'm staying with the traditional "blessed" because it has a sense of divine involvement and because I find it offensive to say to someone who is in mourning, "You should be happy," or, "Congratulations."

When we hear that we are blessed, we should hear as well a sense of responsibility. A blessing given, a talent bestowed, if unappreciated and unused, is wasted.

"Blessed are the poor in spirit, for theirs is the kingdom of heaven"

Luke's alternative (6:20) reads, "Blessed are you who are poor, / for yours is the kingdom of God." Still popular in New Testament studies is the thesis that the authors we call Matthew and Luke had access both to Mark's Gospel, which does not contain the Beatitudes, and to a second hypothetical source, labeled Q from the German word *Quelle* meaning "source." Thought to be the origin of material shared by Luke and Matthew but absent from Mark— material such as the Beatitudes and the Our Father—Q remained a staple of New Testament studies until relatively recently. Having completed a commentary on the Gospel of Luke with my friend, the evangelical scholar Ben Witherington III, I became increasingly doubtful of the existence of Q; it strikes me as just as likely, if not more likely, that Luke had access to Matthew's Gospel.[1]

It is possible that Luke, familiar with Matthew's reading, wanted to put a focus on the economically poor or, since most people in antiquity were poor, those whom we today would identify as destitute. Luke then adds the corresponding "Woe to you who are rich, / for you have received your consolation" (v. 24).

Matthew will have much to say about the rich who allow the poor to starve, go naked, or languish in prison. But here, in the Sermon on the Mount, Matthew keeps the focus on those who require blessing. The woes can wait since comfort should come before condemnation.

Despite the popular view that "poor in spirit" means "weak in faith," that is not what Matthew's phrase means. Nor does it mean simply not being conceited or prideful. "Poor in spirit" is in part a synonym for the people who have enough humility that they do not operate from a sense of pride: the poor in spirit are those who recognize that they are both the beneficiaries of the help of others and part of a system in which they are to pay it forward and help those whom they can. Poor in spirit are those who do *not* sit around saying, "Look at what I've accomplished," or worse, feel resentful because they have not received what they consider sufficient honor. They know they did the right thing; they know God knows, and that's sufficient recognition indeed.

My friend Mike Glenn, a Baptist minister in Brentwood, Tennessee, speaks of the poor in spirit as those who recognize the gap between what we have and what we *should* have. We may have a bank account, but we may not have compassion, generosity, or love. We may have a watertight home, health care, and a car that works, but we may also have neighbors who struggle with paying the rent, putting food on the table, or getting to work. The poor in spirit are those who see what many don't, and they are blessed because they have this vision and because the vision compels them to act. "Mind the gap," says Mike. Spot on.

In talking with friends about the Beatitudes (I'm blessed that my friends put up with me when I want to talk about what a biblical passage means), one asked whether "poor in spirit" could be a coded term for people who have mental health issues. The beatitude is not speaking directly about someone with bipolar disorder or schizophrenia or the various chemical imbalances that create an erroneous reality. But for those who are suffering from such disorders, the Sermon has good news because it demands that the disciples of Jesus pay attention, provide care, and provide love.

The Hebrew word *ani* means "poor" but has the connotation of "those who recognize their dependence on God." Isaiah 66:2 speaks to this idea:

> All these things my hand has made,
> and so all these things are mine,
> says the LORD.
> But this is the one to whom I will look,
> to the humble [*ani*] and contrite in spirit,
> who trembles at my word.

According to the Dead Sea Scroll 1QM (also called the War Scroll), the phrase "poor in spirit" is juxtaposed to the "righteous of God," to those who orient themselves to others and to God and not toward their self-centered concerns.

Thus, "poor in spirit" crosses economic lines. To be poor is not necessarily to be righteous, and if we hold this equation, we wind up romanticizing poverty rather than working to alleviate it. Nor for the Gospels is being rich synonymous with being venal or evil; rather, having surplus comes with the mandate to help others. Matthew mentions several well-off characters, such as the magi with their high-end Christmas gifts of gold, frankincense, and myrrh. Only Matthew's Gospel explicitly identifies Joseph of Arimathea as a "rich man." At the beginning of the mission discourse, Matthew's Jesus tells his disciples, "Take no gold, or silver, or copper in your belts" (10:9). There would have been no need to forbid gold and silver if the disciples didn't have any to take.

My friend, the Baptist author Tony Campolo, got it right. In

February 2008, he told a gathering of fellow Baptists: "There is nothing wrong with making a million dollars. I wish you all would make a million dollars. There is nothing wrong with making it, but there is something wrong with keeping it," he said. "My Bible tells me in 1 John 3:17, 'If anyone has the world's goods and sees his brother in need but shuts off his compassion from him—how can God's love reside in him?'"[2]

If we think of the "poor in spirit" as those who recognize their dependence on others and others' dependence on them, then we can already see how they are blessed. For a modern analogy, the poor in spirit are those who are aware of their own privileges and, because they are aware, work to help others who do not have the same benefits. We who have had the privilege of attending schools with up-to-date materials and motivated teachers might help others who lack such resources. We who have benefited because of the social status of our families, our appearance, contacts, networking, and luck are blessed when we recognize that, no matter our own drive, we did not achieve everything on our own.

Another way we recognize that these individuals are blessed is to acknowledge that Jesus is talking directly to his disciples. *They* are the ones who will not only pray to their Father in heaven (the Our Father is part of the Sermon on the Mount) but also see themselves on earth as part of a family, defined by doing God's will and so engaging in mutual support. Thinking about the disciples, we might pair the Sermon on the Mount with Matthew 12:46-50, where Jesus points to his disciples and says, "Here are my mother and my brothers! For whoever does the will of my Father in heaven is my brother and sister and mother."

I think what Jesus is doing in the Sermon on the Mount is beginning the creation of a new movement with disciples, but not a movement in the way we think of political parties. I think what he's doing is setting up a new family or a new community. How do you live in this group? What would it look like to live in this new family where people actually did what the Sermon on the Mount thinks people should do and where people actually are what the Sermon thinks people should be?

When that support comes, then God's will is done on earth as it is in heaven. Then the disciples can say, "Ours is the kingdom of heaven."

Anyone can be part of this community. I see the Sermon on the Mount as, in part, evoking the Jewish tradition that we are all, in every generation, standing again at Mount Sinai, just as we all, in every generation, imagine ourselves taking off the chains of Egyptian slavery. When Jesus tells his disciples, "Blessed are the poor in spirit, for *theirs* is the kingdom of heaven," he is speaking not just to the few around him on a Galilean mountaintop but across the generations. Theirs *is* the kingdom of heaven—present tense. The poor in spirit don't have to wait until reaching the pearly gates; they already have one foot in that heavenly kingdom today, right now.

"Blessed are those who mourn, for they will be comforted"

Luke's parallel is "Blessed are you who weep now, / for you will laugh" (6:21), and the corresponding woe, absent from the Sermon on the Mount, is "Woe to you who are laughing now, for you will mourn and weep" (v. 25). Luke has a happy/sad focus, whereas Matthew—I think more helpfully—specifies the emotions by speaking of mourning and being comforted. Matthew's version I think comes closer to the heart of what happens in the very real situations of life and death. I also find myself resisting Luke's woe, as I take no comfort when others weep or mourn. Matthew, in the Sermon on the Mount, depicts Jesus as telling his followers, "Love your enemies and pray for those who persecute you" (5:44). I don't think the prayer should be, "I hope your family members die and that you weep as many tears as there are drops in the ocean."

Matthew's verse about mourning comforts me, and the comfort

is found when we unpack the implications of the verse. First, we may conclude that those earlier translations of the Beatitudes with "Happy are you" or "Congratulations to you" are the wrong thing to say when people are mourning. The modern version would be trite and inappropriate sayings: "I'm sure she's in a better place" does not comfort the mourner who may be thinking, *The better place is here, with me.* "God brings home the ones God loves" suggests those of us left here are like chopped liver. "Everything happens for a reason"? No, it does not, and trying to find an explanation for the death of a loved one gets us nowhere.

One of Job's friends says to him, "How happy [*ashrei*] is the one whom God reproves; / therefore do not despise the discipline of the Almighty" (Job 5:17). Job's friend is saying, in effect, "You've been blessed because God is punishing you because of your sins." But Job is innocent, and at the end of the book, God sides with Job against his friends. God sides with the unanswerable mystery of why bad things happen to good people rather than provides an easy answer. If suffering makes us happy, we are not suffering. And if suffering is excused, we are not human.

If I hear again at a funeral that "heaven needed another angel," I may actually throw something. Let's not dismiss mourning, which is what such platitudes try to do. The New Testament takes mourning seriously: Lazarus's sisters mourn him; Jesus's followers mourn him. Death is real. Death is painful. But death, in Judaism and in the Christian church that remembers its Jewish roots, is not the end of the story.

In part those who mourn are blessed because not everyone can mourn. To mourn is to say, "I loved this person, and I desperately miss this person"—a heart that knows how to grieve is a heart that knows how to love.

Next, being able to mourn means being able *to take the time* to mourn and to do so in our own time. In the Jewish tradition, we practice what is called "sitting shiva"—*shiva* is Hebrew for "seven," and the practice takes place not in the synagogue but in the home of the family of the deceased. Shiva, which lasts for seven days, is the time when family members traditionally tear their clothes or wear a torn black ribbon pinned to the clothes; they will sometimes sit on low stools or on the floor. Friends and family come to comfort the mourners (and often bring food). The Kaddish prayer is said as long as a minyan (ten Jews, or in Orthodox families, ten male Jews over the age of thirteen) is present. The Kaddish, a prayer in Aramaic, begins, "Magnified and sanctified be the great Name [of God]," which sounds like "Hallowed be your name."

We don't know, exactly, how the practice originated. I am partial to the early Jewish explanation that it began with Methuselah, the oldest-living human by the biblical account. The time is before the flood. Genesis 7:10 reads, "And after seven days the waters of the flood came on the earth," and Rashi, the medieval Jewish commentator, explains, "These are the seven days of mourning for the righteous man Methuselah for whose honor the Holy One, blessed be He, had regard."[3] The message is this: death comes to everyone. Alternatively, Genesis 50:10 tells us that Joseph, in Egypt, "observed a time of mourning for his father [the patriarch Jacob] seven days." Still one more explanation comes from Job 2:13, where Job's friends, hearing of the death of Job's children and wife and the devastations of his body, "sat with him on the ground seven days and seven nights." Whatever the explanation, the tradition allows the family to mourn, as their friends come to comfort not by offering platitudes but by offering memory and story and presence.

Jewish mourning customs take the family through the next year and into the future. On the anniversary of the loved one's death, the family lights a *yahrzeit* (Yiddish: "year time") candle in memory. The week of the anniversary of the person's death, calculated according to the Jewish calendar, the rabbi reads aloud the person's name, and so the memory is kept alive also in the community. It is traditional to make a charitable donation in memory.

The beatitude has a particular resonance for Jesus's followers that also draws from the Jewish tradition. Isaiah 61:1-4, the passage Jesus partially cites as part of his address to the Nazareth synagogue in Luke 4, reads,

> The spirit of the Lord GOD is upon me,
>   because the LORD has anointed me;
> he has sent me to bring good news to the oppressed,
>   to bind up the brokenhearted,
> to proclaim liberty to the captives,
>   and release to the prisoners;
> to proclaim the year of the LORD's favor,
>   and the day of vengeance of our God;
>   to comfort all who mourn;
> to provide for those who mourn in Zion—
>   to give them a garland instead of ashes,
> the oil of gladness instead of mourning,
>   the mantle of praise instead of a faint spirit.
> They will be called oaks of righteousness,
>   the planting of the LORD, to display his glory.
> They shall build up the ancient ruins,
>   they shall raise up the former devastations;
> they shall repair the ruined cities,
>   the devastations of many generations.

Isaiah, writing at the end of the Babylonian exile, announces how redemption comes on the communal level. His specific concern is the rebuilding of Jerusalem.

He comforts the mourners in Zion by telling them that theirs is not the last generation, that what they may not see to fruition, their children and their children's children will. To mourn in Israel means that we are not alone; we have not only our friends and relatives but also the previous generations and the generations to come. And we take comfort in that.

Since Isaiah is also a prophet, we can add more to this idea of mourning and being comforted. Those who mourn, if we read with Isaiah, are those who also mourned the sins that led to destruction.

They mourned the failure of many in the community to think in terms of, to quote Jesus, "Your will be done, on earth as it is in heaven." They mourned the failure of people to get to the heart of Torah, to avoid anger as well as murder, lust before adultery.

We can mourn for many things: the death of a loved one, yes. But we also mourn for the abused child, the victims of the latest terrorist attack, our veterans who gave their lives in defense of our country. And we should take comfort in the fact that we care—because not all do.

There are yet two more readings of this beatitude that arise from its placement in Matthew's Gospel. First, Jesus is speaking to his disciples, and it will be his followers who become the first readers of the Gospel. Jesus tells his followers, "The wedding guests cannot mourn as long as the bridegroom is with them, can they? The days will come when the bridegroom is taken away from them, and then they will fast" (Matthew 9:15). The disciples will mourn Jesus, murdered on a Roman cross. But they will be comforted because they will see him, according to Matthew, on a mountaintop in Galilee, resurrected. Thus Matthew's Gospel itself shows both the mourning and the comfort.

Second, toward the end of the Christmas story, Matthew reports how Herod the Great slaughters all the children, ages two and under, in Bethlehem in order to kill baby Jesus. Matthew glosses this scene by reporting,

> Then was fulfilled what had been spoken through the prophet Jeremiah:
>
> "A voice was heard in Ramah,
>   wailing and loud lamentation,
> Rachel weeping for her children;
>   she refused to be consoled, because they are no more."
>
> Matthew 2:17-18

Here's why knowledge of the Scriptures of Israel is essential for understanding the Gospel, for Matthew is quoting Jeremiah

31, the famous "New Covenant" chapter. Jeremiah is known as the "prophet of consolation," and his entire book can be summarized by Matthew's second beatitude. Jeremiah's next verses (16-17) are God's response to Rachel and, by extension, to all of us who mourn:

> Thus says the LORD:
> Keep your voice from weeping,
>   and your eyes from tears;
> for there is a reward for your work,
>   says the LORD:
>   they shall come back from the land of the enemy;
> there is hope for your future,
>   says the LORD:
>   your children shall come back to their own country.

Matthew's readers, then and now, knowing this connection to Jeremiah, will see Rachel's hope for the resurrection of those children.

Finally, my preferred comment to those who are in mourning, and the one that meant the most to me when my father died and then my mother, is "May his [or her] memory be for a blessing." My father died when I was thirteen; I was devastated. I was able, however, to find comfort in that greeting, since it reminded me that I carried his legacy with me. We bless the memories of the dead when we tell the stories: your dad made this crib for my baby, your mom knitted this afghan, your dad taught me how to bake, your mom taught me how to drive.

We bless the memories even when they bring to mind our own regrets: *I should have told her . . . I should have said . . .* Somehow, they know.

Finally, how we act has repercussions for their memory. How I acted could bring honor to the memory of my parents. I shall always be Saul Levine's daughter (my daughter Sarah is named after him) and Anne Levine's daughter. I still talk to them, despite the fact that my father died in 1970 and my mother in 1994. They are always with me, and their memory remains for a blessing.

What we do, in the memory of those who are no longer with us in the body, keeps that memory alive, honors the dead, and in the very actions we perform, we receive comfort.

"Blessed are the meek, for they will . . ."

There is no Lucan parallel here—perhaps Luke recognized that there was no reason to repeat this beatitude, since it is a direct quote from the Scriptures of Israel. Psalm 37:11 reads, "But the meek shall inherit the land, and delight themselves in abundant prosperity." The Hebrew translated here as "the meek" is *anawim*, our synonym for "poor in spirit."

But we can do more with the term *meek* given the nuances of the Greek term Matthew uses, *praus*. This is the word the Septuagint uses to describe Moses in Numbers 12:3, translated by the NRSV as "Now the man Moses was very humble, more so than anyone else on the face of the earth." Given that Moses is the traditional author of the Book of Numbers, I have always found this verse marvelously ironic, as if Moses is saying, "Look at how humble I am."

The term shows up later in Matthew 11:29, in Jesus's self-reference: "Take my yoke upon you, and learn from me; for I am gentle [*praus*] and humble in heart." Jesus is not saying he is insignificant, so "meek" has to mean something else. We find it again in Matthew 21:5, the "triumphal entry," in a quotation from Zechariah:

> "Tell the daughter of Zion,
> Look, your king is coming to you,
>   humble [*praus*], and mounted on a donkey,
>   and on a colt, the foal of a donkey."

From these other uses, we can tell that "meek" in the beatitude does not mean "insignificant compared to you." To the contrary, a meek person is a person with great authority, but one who does not lord it over others. A meek person promotes servant leadership over despotism.

The epitome of the meek king is Jesus, and not just because of the entry on the donkey. (Solomon rode a mule in 1 Kings 1:38, and Solomon was not known for his limited ego.) The model of the meek king is the beginning of what is known as the "Christ Hymn" of Paul's Epistle to the Philippians (2:6-11). The hymn (which may be a liturgical formula meant to be recited, not sung) describes the Christ:

> Though he was in the form of God,
>> did not regard equality with God
>> as something to be exploited,
> but emptied himself,
>> taking the form of a slave,
>> being born in human likeness.
> And being found in human form,
>> he humbled himself
>> and became obedient to the point of death—
>> even death on a cross. (vv. 6-8)

The Greek term the NRSV translates as "humbled" is not our term, *praus*, but the verb *tapeinoō*, a term found two other times in Matthew to make the same point about the nonexploitative, dependent life: "Whoever becomes humble like this child is the greatest in the kingdom of heaven" (18:4), and "All who exalt themselves will be humbled, and all who humble themselves will be exalted" (23:12).

We have from antiquity, in both Jewish and pagan sources, a number of stories about so-called meek rulers. Here are two quick examples:

Cassius Dio, the Roman historian of the late second or early third century, writes in his *Roman History* (69.6.3) about a woman who makes a request of the emperor Hadrian. He responds, "I haven't time." The woman counters, "Cease, then, being Emperor." Her ploy works. Dio explains, "This is a kind of preface, of a summary nature, that I have been giving in regard to his character" (69.8.1).[4]

The Babylonian Talmud, a compendium of Jewish lore and law from the first several centuries CE, recounts how Rabbi Judah the Prince, the man responsible for the codification of the first compendium of rabbinic law, the Mishnah, learned meekness from a fellow rabbi. As the story goes, during a time of famine, Rabbi Judah determined to provide food only to those who were educated in the Jewish texts. Rabbi Jonathan ben Amram, in disguise, then demanded that he be given food. Rabbi Judah resisted because he was unconvinced that this apparently unlearned man was deserving. But Rabbi Jonathan responded, "Sustain me like a dog and like a raven, who are given food even though they have not learned anything" (we can hear an anticipation of Jesus's reference to the ravens in the Sermon on the Mount). Rabbi Judah then provided him some food.

But Rabbi Judah's conscience troubled him—how could he give bread to someone who had not learned the Scriptures? Then his son said to him, "Perhaps he was your disciple [Jonathan] ben Amram, who never in his life wanted to materially benefit from the honor shown to the Torah." Rabbi Judah checked, and sure enough, he learned Rabbi Jonathan was the beggar in disguise. And so he concluded, "Let everyone enter" (Bava Batra 8a).

Through his persistence, Rabbi Jonathan taught Rabbi Judah how to be meek: how to listen—really listen—to those in need, how to share resources, how to realize that he did not know everything.

These examples of meek kings, and of people in authority who do not rely on that authority to boss others around, are very good examples for people in similar social situations today. For a CEO to practice humility is an appropriate exercise. However, to tell that CEO's office worker, who works two jobs, barely makes minimum wage, and is struggling to care for both elderly parents and little children, to have a bit more humility is probably not the right advice. For some people—those who have been told they are worthless, those who feel themselves failures, those who can barely keep their heads above water—the instruction to give up any sense of self can do damage. Jesus is speaking to his disciples, the privileged, the ones who own boats or land or homes. Not all ears will hear the beatitude the same way; what is a blessing to one may be, if heard incorrectly, a curse to another.

". . . inherit the earth"

Given that the original psalm proclaims that the meek will "inherit the land," we need to address why Matthew's text speaks of inheriting the earth. The solution to this mystery is the translator's choice. Both the Hebrew term *eretz* and its Greek translation *gē* (as in geology) mean both "earth" and "land." The translators of the Psalm chose "land" (which has the connotation of the land of Israel); the translators of Matthew's Greek chose "earth." Both translations have something to teach us. "Land" reminds us of how meekness can help in border disputes; "earth" reminds us how meekness can help in protecting the planet. "Land" concerns one's homeland; "earth" concerns the globe.

Another psalm, also concerned about inheriting and land, helps us draw out the implications of these various texts. Psalm 37:29 reads, "The righteous shall inherit the land, / and live in it forever." *Righteousness*, as we will see, is one of Matthew's favorite words. So I asked Matthew—Matthew and I have been having frequent conversations since I wrote my dissertation on this Gospel back in 1984—"Did you intend an allusion to this psalm as well?" He replied, "Good job, AJ; I can see where you get this." Matthew loves to make allusions to the Scriptures of Israel; the Gospel offers one verse, and immediately we are reminded of several others.

Inheriting the earth, or the land, is not a windfall; it is a responsibility. To be the heir of something means that we have been given something treasured. Our job is to be a good steward of that legacy. God created the heavens and the earth at the beginning of creation. God gave the earth into the care of humanity for us to fill it and subdue it (Genesis 1:28). The point is not to strip it of its resources any more than we should strip the gold from our great-grandmother's wedding ring.

If we inherit the land but use it entirely for our own benefit, we are not treating it responsibly or according to the wishes of the one who bequeathed it to us. Nor can we inherit the earth if there's nothing left: the mountains stripped of their tops, the oceans filled with plastic, the air choked with pollutants. Only the meek, those who would not use the inheritance to reinforce their own already privileged position, are worthy to care for the land. They understand stewardship, they understand restriction of activity (for what one *can* do is not necessarily what one *should* do), and they understand their responsibility in turn to pass the land to others.

Moving on from the Beatitudes

Books have been written on each of the Beatitudes. We have barely covered three, and still to come are the blessings on those who "hunger and thirst for righteousness," the merciful, the pure in heart, the peacemakers, those who are persecuted for the sake of righteousness, and the disciples of Jesus, who will be reviled because others do not understand their commitment to the gospel.

If we reflect on the first three beatitudes, we can already see hints of how to understand the next six. Those who hunger and thirst for righteousness are those who understand dependence and obligation, loss and memory, power and responsibility. To demand righteousness, which is related, linguistically, to the term for "justice," should also bring us to mercy. Justice without mercy is intolerable, but mercy without justice is equally intolerable: actions must have consequences. The pure in heart are those who have sloughed off the clutter, the distractions, of the world: money and fame and power and status. Peacemakers will inevitably be persecuted, for they inevitably ask parties to sacrifice for the greater good.

On those who find themselves having others "utter all kinds

of evil" against them on account of Jesus or who suffer for carrying the name "Christian," Jesus is not talking about the so-called war on Christmas, what decorations appear on the winter-season coffee cup, or whether the mall rings with sounds of "Happy holidays" rather than "Merry Christmas." This is not persecution. This is respect for those who do not identify as Christian. Jesus's concern is that one welcome the strangers, not hit them over the head with candy canes and tinsel. He is rather aware of those who risk their lives to live the gospel. In parts of the world, the practice of Christianity is illegal, churches are bombed, and children are hounded. To be aware of this persecution should prompt his followers to risk their reputations to make peace when others in their neighborhoods—the people without the tree in the living room or the lights by the door—are persecuted for being different.

We can leave the Beatitudes with the phrase "blessed are" ringing in our ears. We could attempt to recite all nine (there should be a mnemonic, but I've yet to hear one I've remembered), but perhaps a better exercise is to continue the pattern and develop our own. Blessed are those who care for broken bodies or lonely children, blessed are those who sit by the dying at night, blessed are those who can sing of God asking "Whom shall I send?" and can respond "It is I Lord. . . . I have heard you calling in the night." The path is narrow and the journey hard, but the blessings are found in every step forward.

Chapter 2

THE EXTENSIONS

False Charges and an Eloquent Defense

Having climbed a mountain and sat down, Jesus begins to teach his disciples. The crowds, at a distance, are listening. He begins with the Beatitudes, words of encouragement concerning the human condition, and words of assurance that proper attitudes and the compassionate actions that flow from them both are blessings and create blessings. The last of the nine beatitudes is one particular to those who worship Jesus: "Blessed are you when people revile you and persecute you and utter all kinds of evil against you falsely on my account" (Matthew 5:11). As the Sermon goes on, we find one of the major charges leveled against Jesus and his followers, and Jesus's rejection of it. Once we fill in the accusation, we can then see just how profound the extensions, which make up the next major section of the Sermon on the Mount, actually are.

Jesus announces, "Do not think that I have come to abolish the law or the prophets; I have come not to abolish but to fulfill. For truly [the Greek actually says *amen*] I tell you, until heaven and earth pass away, not one letter, not one stroke of a letter, will pass from the law until all is accomplished" (5:17-18). Although *amen* (a Hebrew term meaning "so be it" from the root meaning "to be confirmed, reliable, ever faithful") typically ends a prayer, Jesus often begins his statements with this term. He is sanctioning his remarks even before he speaks them. When Jesus utters an "amen" before a statement, we do well to pay attention.

He tells his followers in this section that they should be more righteousness than the Pharisees—a bar set high, not low. To be a disciple means to follow Torah, and it means, therefore, to follow Jesus's Torah instruction. If the disciple doesn't bear good fruits, then the system doesn't work.

The reference to "letter" is, in Greek, the word *iota*, the name of the smallest letter in the Greek alphabet. The underlying Hebrew would be *yod*. That term along with the word for "stroke" is where the King James Version translates "one jot or one tittle." "Jot," which comes from the Greek *iota*, appears in colloquial English when we "jot that down" (that is, make a short note). Tittle is the dot over the lowercase letters *i* and *j*.

By "law" Jesus is speaking of the Torah, the five books of Moses. Although the Hebrew term *Torah* enters into the Greek as *nomos*, translated "law," the Hebrew is better translated "instruction." Prophets are the former prophets (1–2 Samuel; 1–2 Kings), major prophets (Isaiah, Jeremiah, and Ezekiel), and twelve minor prophets (minor not because they are less important; minor because the books are comparably shorter). These texts together especially with the Psalms, ground Jesus's teachings, become the charter for the Gentile communities Paul founds, and are the bedrock of both Judaism and Christianity.

When Jesus speaks of fulfilling this material, he is not suggesting that once he says or does something related to the ancient text, that text can be regarded as both checked off and checked out. To the contrary, or as Paul would say, "No way!" (This often comes into English as "By no means!" as in Romans 7:13.) Jesus asserts that the Scripture of Israel remains sacred for his followers. When Jesus speaks of "fulfilling" the Torah, he signals that he is drawing out its full implications.

Jesus discussed Torah with fellow Jews. As far as I can tell, pretty much all Jews then and now discussed Torah. He never dismissed it; he never transgressed it. We do know that Paul was charged, incorrectly, with dismissing Torah. By placing these words about the permanence of the Torah on Jesus's lips, Matthew corrects any readers who might have thought otherwise, then and now.

A Brief Note on Paul and Torah

Most Jews, including Paul, did not think that pagans needed to convert to Judaism. Jews spoke of the seven laws given to Noah after the flood. Summarized in various places, one version from the Babylonian Talmud, Sanhedrin 56a, enjoins upon all of Noah's descendants the following *mitzvot* ("commandments," but with the connotation of "good deeds"): (1) to establish just courts, (2) to refrain from cursing the name of God, (3) to avoid idol worship, (4) to avoid illicit sexual activities, (5) to refrain from murder, (6) to refrain from robbery, and (7) never to eat the limb of a living animal.

Nothing here about circumcision, avoiding pork or shellfish, celebrating the Sabbath, or making pilgrimage to the Jerusalem Temple. When Paul brought the gospel to the pagans, he does not tell them to observe the Sabbath (in the seven letters all biblical scholars agree that Paul wrote, he makes no mention of the Sabbath), and he warns the pagan men against circumcising themselves.

Paul insists that he is the apostle to the Gentiles, and so his letters are written to Gentiles. But rumors started that Paul was discouraging Jews from following the very mitzvot that distinguished Jews from the rest of the empire (today, we would call this multiculturalism). Paul was not against the Torah. He was against pagans converting to Judaism. For Paul, the messianic age—which he saw as beginning with the Christ's resurrection—had begun, and in that messianic age, Jews and Gentiles both worshipped the God of Israel. Were the pagans to convert to Judaism, then only Jews would be part of that grand chorus.

The So-Called Antitheses

"You have heard that it was said to those of ancient times,
'You shall not murder'; and 'whoever murders shall be liable
to judgment.' But I say to you that if you are angry with a
brother or sister, you will be liable to judgment; and if you
insult a brother or sister, you will be liable to the council;
and if you say, 'You fool,' you will be liable to the hell of fire."

Matthew 5:21-22

Although this verse sounds like an antithesis, it is not. Jesus is
not opposing Torah; he is extending it.

As noted in our opening chapter, Matthew presents Jesus as a
new Moses, and so it is appropriate that from the mountaintop he
provides his understanding of the Torah Moses gave to Israel on
Mount Sinai. In each case, beginning with some variant on the formula "You have heard it said . . . but I say to you," Jesus extends, in-
tensifies, and glosses the commandments. To the command against
murder, he adds the forbidding of anger. An antithesis would be:
"You have heard that it was said to those of ancient times, 'You shall
not murder'; and 'whoever murders shall be liable to judgment'; but
I say to you: 'lock and load.'"

Along with the injunction against murder and so anger, Jesus
offers five more teachings:

1. To the command against adultery, he adds the forbidding
   of lust.
2. To instructions on how to divorce, Jesus tightens the mar-
   ital bond by permitting divorce only in the case of *porneia*,
   a Greek term that will be discussed later.
3. To the commandment against taking a false oath, Jesus
   forbids oath-taking.
4. To the famous "an eye for an eye," Jesus changes the
   subject.
5. And to the commandment about loving the neighbor, he
   insists that disciples must love their enemies.

Despite the evocation of Moses, Jesus is not reading from a text. Nevertheless, Matthew sets out a lovely rhetorical balance. Biblical scholar Ulrich Luz notes that the first three teachings have 1,131 letters in Greek, and the last two have 1,130.[1]

We shall not have time to look at all these extensions, but by looking at a representative example, we shall see how Jesus fulfills Torah—he fulfills it by getting to the core values of the commandments. By following the commandments, as Jesus interprets them, his disciples walk as if they have one foot already in the kingdom of heaven.

Building a Fence Around Murder: Forbidding Anger

The first extension begins, "You have heard that it was said to those of ancient times" (5:21) followed by the commandment itself "'You shall not murder'" (5:21). The commandment, found in Exodus 20:13 and Deuteronomy 5:17, is part of the Ten Commandments or Decalogue (Greek for "ten words" or by extension, "ten teachings"). The Hebrew root behind this commandment is *r-tz-ch*, and it refers to intentional killing or murder. The King James Version translation, "Thou shalt not kill," is too general.

The second phrase, "whoever murders shall be liable to judgment," is not a quotation but a paraphrase. "Liable to judgment," a vague but ominous threat, likely refers to Genesis 9:6, where God tells Noah, "Whoever sheds the blood of a human, / by a human shall that person's blood be shed." The Decalogue, along with other biblical passages, takes homicide to be a capital offense (see especially Numbers 35:16-18).

On the other hand, the Bible as well as postbiblical Judaism both consistently undercut the idea of capital punishment. Whereas God tells Noah that murder should be punished by death, only five chapters earlier, in Genesis 4, God protected Cain, who killed his brother Abel. Similarly, although Moses committed murder (Exodus 2:12), he is not executed; instead, he liberates Israel from slavery. As with today's legal system, what the law mandates on the ideal level is not necessarily what occurs in practice.

Moreover, biblical law itself deconstructs. After telling Noah the consequences of shedding blood, God then says, "For in his own image / God made humankind." The problem: people who commit murder *are also* in the image of God; once we recognize that they are also in the divine image, we need to come up with a response other than execution.

Jesus offers his extension: "But I say to you that if you are angry with a brother or sister [that is, a community member], you will be liable to judgment; and if you insult a brother or sister, you will be liable to the council [Greek: *sanhedrin*, meaning the local court]; and if you say, 'You fool,' you will be liable to the hell of fire" (Matthew 5:22).

Jesus is talking about how disciples are to live. His immediate audience comprises (at least) Simon (to be named Peter) and Andrew, James and John, individuals who left their homes to join him. Jesus is setting up an ideal community—anthropologists would call this a "fictive kinship unit"—where the group members replace the natal family's mother and brothers and sisters. The group has only one father, the one who is in heaven.

The communities gathered in Jesus's name had procedures designed for disciplining recalcitrant members. For example, Matthew 18:15-17 prescribes a formal process for reprimand that is followed, if necessary, by a removal from fellowship: speak to the person individually; if that doesn't work, send a committee. If that doesn't work, the individual who refuses to accept community reconciliation is to be treated "as a Gentile and a tax collector" (v. 17), that is, someone to be (re-)evangelized and encouraged to repent.

Jesus's extension, meant to convey the seriousness of angry words, does what rabbinic Judaism calls "building a fence around the Torah." The expression comes from the Mishnaic tractate *Pirke*

Avot, or as we noted in the introduction, the Rabbis' greatest hits. Avot opens, "Moses received Torah at Sinai and handed it on to Joshua, Joshua to elders, and elders to prophets. And prophets handed it on to the men of the great assembly. They said three things: Be prudent in judgment. Raise up many disciples. Make a fence for the Torah." As a fence around a house protects what is inside, so the fence around the Torah protects the commandments by creating the circumstances that make violation more difficult. If one is not angry, one is less likely to commit murder.

A few scribes copying the text of Matthew 5 recognized that in some cases anger is justified—what we would call "righteous anger"—and they added to Matthew's verse the exception "angry *without cause*." I agree with this gloss. If we are not made angry by suffering, by cheating, by indifference, then we are not human.

Now, should an earthly court fail to provide appropriate punishment, the heavenly judge will: hence the "hell" (Greek: *gehenna*) reference (v. 22). We find a similar saying in the Babylonian Talmud Berakhot 19a, where Rabbi Yehoshua ben Levi proposes excommunicating a disciple for insulting his teacher: "One who speaks disparagingly after the biers of Torah scholars and maligns them after their death will fall in Gehenna, as it is stated, 'But those who turn aside unto their crooked ways, the Lord will lead them away with the workers of iniquity; peace be upon Israel'" (citing Psalm 125:5). I have thought of including this statement on my syllabi.

Neither Jesus nor the rabbis necessarily, or even clearly, believed in hell in the sense of a place of eternal torment. The Scriptures of Israel do not have a well-developed sense of an afterlife; they tend to speak of Sheol (the "pit") where the dead went—both those who cared for the poor, the widow, the orphan, and the stranger and those who cared only for themselves.

Ezekiel speaks of Israel's resurrection: "As I prophesied, suddenly there was a noise, a rattling, and the bones came together, bone to its bone. I looked, and there were sinews on them, and flesh had come upon them, and skin had covered them, but there was no breath in them" (Ezekiel 37:7-8) This becomes not only the origin of the song "Dem Bones" but also a prompt for personal resurrection.

Under Persian and then Greek and Roman influence, Jewish views of the afterlife developed. The Book of Daniel, likely composed in the mid-second century BCE, proclaims, "Many of those who sleep in the dust of the earth shall awake, some to everlasting life, and some to shame and everlasting contempt" (Daniel 12:2). Everlasting life sounds like eternal life, and most Jews at the time of Jesus believed in resurrection of the dead, a teaching promoted by the Pharisees.

"Shame and everlasting contempt" is not the same thing as Dante's *Inferno*. The point is not eternal torture; it is a lasting memory. Even those sent "into the eternal fire" (Matthew 25:41) do not suffer forever. The fire continues, but sinners are reduced to dust and ashes. Jesus assures his disciples, "Do not fear those who kill the body but cannot kill the soul; rather fear him who can destroy both soul and body in hell [Gehenna]" (Matthew 10:28). The punishment is not eternal torture but annihilation or oblivion.

Before we leave this extension—and there is so much more I want to talk about—just a final word on name-calling. Jesus sees connections between murder and insult, death and name-calling. He's right. We've heard that "Sticks and stones can break my bones, but names can never hurt me," but the saying is wrong. Names hurt. Names kill. In our call-out culture, children are cyberbullied to death; people take their lives because of the barrage of insults. Names kill. Jesus was right; if we would only listen to him.

Building a Fence Around Adultery: Forbidding Lust

Our second intensification appears in 5:27-28: "You have heard that it was said, 'You shall not commit adultery.' But I say to you that everyone who looks at a woman with lust has already committed adultery with her in his heart." Jesus is citing Exodus 20:14 and Deuteronomy 5:18. Leviticus 20:10 notes the punishment: "If a man commits adultery with the wife of his neighbor, both the adulterer and the adulteress shall be put to death."

Adultery in this context—Israel was a polygynous society— means sexual relations between a married or a betrothed woman and a man other than her husband or betrothed. Today, adultery is infidelity by either spouse. At the time of Jesus, a Jewish man could have sexual relations with a divorcée, a prostitute, or an otherwise unmarried and unengaged woman: it might not look nice, but it was not forbidden. (We might compare the dating habits of the American teenager—but we won't.)

Whether Jews in the Second Temple period were executing people guilty of adultery remains an open question, and as far as I can determine, they were not. Israel's Scriptures contain no examples of such execution. David and Bathsheba provide the most notable example of adultery (2 Samuel 11), and neither is executed. However, the son conceived from their adulterous relation dies (2 Samuel 12:18), so God carries out a vicarious punishment. Hosea (1:2-9) depicts his marriage to an adulterous wife, but the relationship prompts reconciliation, not death. Indeed, the prophetic metaphor of Israel as an adulterous spouse does not lead to Israel's death but to shame, repentance, and ultimately reconciliation with God.

The story of Susanna, an appendix to the Book of Daniel and one of the world's first detective stories, depicts a woman facing execution on the false charge of adultery. She is rescued when Daniel, who conveniently shows up, demonstrates that the elders who accused her were lying. This fictional account shows Daniel's wisdom, not historical judicial procedure.

John's story of the woman caught in adultery does not presume execution. This account, which begins to appear in New Testament manuscripts from the fourth century, depicts no court case, and the procedures are at best incomplete. The story lacks reference to, let alone appearance of, the man with whom the accused was said to commit adultery. A woman cannot commit adultery on her own. Further complicating any formal legal process, there is no eyewitness testimony.

John's story does not presume that people are being executed for adultery. To the contrary, Jesus's opponents seek to trap him by asking what he would do regarding this guilty woman. If he says, "Execute her," they will condemn him of barbarism or of failing to follow court procedure. If he says, "Release her," they will condemn him for transgressing biblical law. Jesus then asks his opponents about their qualifications for judging: "Let anyone among you who is without sin be the first to throw a stone at her" (John 8:7). The opponents, defeated, leave. The account ends not with Jesus's forgiving the woman but rather with his warning, "Do not sin again" (v. 11).

Also suggesting the lack of capital punishment in cases of adultery is Matthew's nativity account. When Joseph learns that his betrothed, Mary, is pregnant, he decides to divorce her quietly (1:19). Mary is not in danger of stoning, and Matthew makes no mention of public shaming.

The Talmud gives adultery an entire tractate, called Sotah in reference to the "test of bitter waters" given to a wife whose husband suspects her of infidelity (Numbers 5:11-31). Yet the Talmud goes out of its way to make execution for adultery difficult. The rabbis insist, for example, not only that the adulterous act be observed by two witnesses (most adultery, as far as I am aware, is not done in public) but also that the couple be warned in advance that their actions could lead to the death penalty. In effect, the rabbis build a fence around the death penalty: they make the legal procedures so rigorous that executing the guilty party becomes almost impossible.

The rabbis generally sought to prevent the death penalty. For example, Deuteronomy 21:18-21 required that a rebellious son be stoned; the Mishnah Sanhedrin 8 makes the rules so stringent for stoning that son that it is virtually impossible to fulfill them. Another Mishnah (Makkot 1:10) notes how rare capital punishment was: "A sanhedrin that executes once in seven years, is called murderous. Rabbi Eleazar b. Azariah says: once in seventy years. Rabbi Tarfon and Rabbi Akiva say: 'Had we been members of a sanhedrin, no person would ever be put to death.'"[2]

Although adultery does not appear to have been a capital crime in late Second Temple Judaism, it was still a serious problem. Jesus builds the fence by equating (male) lust with adultery: "But I say to you that everyone who looks at a woman with lust has already committed adultery with her in his heart" (Matthew 5:28). The term for "lust" or "desire" (Greek: *epithymeō*) appears in the Septuagint's rendition of the Ten Commandments in forbidding the coveting of the neighbor's house, as well as wife (Exodus 20:17; Deuteronomy 5:21).

Lust is thus a form of greed: the desire to possess what belongs to someone else. The text does treat women as a commodity, as objects of desire, which is another manifestation of that same double standard we saw in the definition of adultery. I wonder: the New Revised Standard Version translates Matthew 5:22 inclusively: "If you are angry with a brother or sister . . . if you insult a brother or sister . . ." even though the Greek text does not mention the sisters. Why then does it offer for 5:28, "Everyone who looks at a woman with lust has already committed adultery with her" rather than "Everyone who looks a person with lust has already committed adultery with that person"? Lust is not a sin reserved for heterosexual males.

Jesus then extends or fence-builds with the hyperbolic command: "If your right eye causes you to sin, tear it out and throw it away; it is better for you to lose one of your members than for your whole body to be thrown into hell" (5:29). At the least, thoughts of physical mutilation should put a damper on sexual desire.

Building a Fence Around Divorce: Forbidding Remarriage

Continuing the theme of proper sexual activity, Jesus alludes to Deuteronomy 24:1-4:

Suppose a man enters into marriage with a woman, but she does not please him because he finds something objectionable [Hebrew: 'ervat davar] about her, and so he writes her a certificate of divorce, puts it in her hand, and sends her out of his house; she then leaves his house and goes off to become another man's wife. Then suppose the second man dislikes her, writes her a bill of divorce, puts it in her hand, and sends her out of his house (or the second man who married her dies); her first husband, who sent her away, is not permitted to take her again to be his wife after she has been defiled; for that would be abhorrent to the LORD, and you shall not bring guilt on the land that the LORD your God is giving you as a possession.

It takes a scorecard to follow the progress of this law. The bottom line is that a divorced woman, after remarriage, cannot return to her first husband. The woman is not "defiled" or "unclean" in general but only in terms of relations with that first husband.

Since marriage was a covenant—that is, a contractual relationship—in ancient Israel, paperwork needed to be drawn up in order to dissolve the relationship. The certificate of divorce is called, in Hebrew, a *get*.

In the first century and into rabbinic literature, Jews debated the meaning of Deuteronomy 24. The more common view at the time was the more restricted view: only adultery was grounds for divorce. As rabbinic Judaism developed, restrictions on divorce lessened. On the one hand, a form of no-fault system became introduced; on the other, Jewish women had marriage contracts (Hebrew: *ketubah*) that, much like a prenuptial agreement, provided them economic support in case of a divorce.

According to the Mishnah (Gittin 9:10), the House of Shammai takes 'ervat davar to refer to adultery (indicating also that no one is stoned for adultery) and makes divorce permissible only on that ground. The House of Hillel takes a basically no-fault position. I'm not much liking Rabbi Akiva, representing the House of Hillel here, especially since, as legend has it, his wife made major sacrifices so that he could study the sacred texts. On the other hand, both schools recognized the *ketubah*, the wife's financial protection in case of divorce.

Taking the conservative position, Jesus extends it from remarrying the first wife to forbidding both divorce and remarriage. He begins, "It was also said, 'Whoever divorces his wife, let him give her a certificate of divorce'" (Matthew 5:31); he then extends the law to forbidding any remarriage: "But I say to you that anyone who divorces his wife, except on the ground of unchastity [Greek: *logou porneias*], causes her to commit adultery; and whoever marries a divorced woman commits adultery" (5:32; compare 19:1-12).

Mark and Luke have the same statement but without the *porneia* exception clause. Similarly, Paul tells his Gentile congregants in Corinth: "To the married I give this command—not I but the Lord—that the wife should not separate from her husband (but if she does separate, let her remain unmarried or else be reconciled to her husband), and that the husband should not divorce his wife" (1 Corinthians 7:10-11). Matthew may have added the reference to *porneia*, perhaps supposing that was Jesus's intent or perhaps recognizing that, since the end of the world had not come as early as Mark and Paul expected, members of the congregation trapped in irreparably broken relationships needed relief.

I've provided both the Hebrew and the Greek because the terms are frustratingly vague. The Hebrew behind "something objectionable" or "a matter of impropriety" is not necessarily sexual. The same phrase, *'ervat davar*, appears in Deuteronomy 23:14 in the context of digging trenches for latrines. The term thus concerns something unpleasant or disgusting.

The "matter of *porneia*" signals vagueness: *porneia* is related to the modern term "pornography," a notoriously difficult term to define. As Supreme Court Justice Potter Stewart said in *Jacobellis v. Ohio* (1964) on defining "hard-core" pornography, "I know it when I see it." The problem is that pornography to one person might be high art to another. Matthew's *porneia* might refer to an incestuous relationship, an illegal one (for example, the wife was already married to someone else), a marriage in which one partner was unfaithful, or even an act of lewdness (variously defined).

Contrary to popular teaching, Jesus's forbidding of divorce is not designed to protect women from husbands issuing arbitrary divorce decrees, a point made obvious from Mark's forbidding a wife from divorcing her husband and remarrying (Mark 10:12). Jesus grounds his teaching not in social reform but in Genesis. To see how he does this, we move from the Sermon on the Mount to Matthew 19. There, some Pharisees, seeking to "test" him (we'll come back to this term in the next chapter when we speak about the Our Father prayer), ask, "Is it lawful for a man to divorce his wife for any cause?" (19:3). That was, in fact, the question of the day.

Jesus responds, not by citing social engineering, women's rights, or the latest poll. He is not trying to protect women from being tossed out onto the streets; he did not need to, for the *ketubah* already protected her. He responds by citing Genesis: "Have you not read that the one who made them at the beginning 'made them male and female.' . . . 'For this reason a man shall leave his father and mother and be joined to his wife, and the two shall become one flesh'? So they are no longer two, but one flesh. Therefore, what God has joined together, let no one separate" (19:4-6).

When the Pharisees then ask why Deuteronomy includes instructions on the *get*, the certificate of divorce, Jesus responds, "It was because you were so hard-hearted that Moses allowed you to divorce your wives, but from the beginning it was not so." Then he repeats, "Whoever divorces his wife, except for unchastity [*porneia*], and marries another commits adultery" (19:8-9).

The disciples are understandably worried. They figure that if marriage is permanent, then it might be better not to make the initial commitment. Jesus responds, cryptically, by noting that not all have the gift of celibacy, not all have disinterest in fathering children.

These teachings raise serious questions for disciples who feel the need to divorce, for marriages, then and now, break down. Paul, who knows Jesus's teaching on divorce, states, "If the unbelieving partner separates, let it be so; in such a case the brother or sister is not bound. It is to peace that God has called you" (1 Corinthians 7:15). A marriage that looks like a battlefield is not a marriage sanctioned by God.

The term *porneia* is sufficiently vague to encompass a host of problems, as is the Hebrew *'ervat davar.* Perhaps into this category falls not only infidelity but also desertion, spousal abuse, loss of affection, the coming to terms with a person's sexuality or gender identity (for example, homosexual or transgender people who married because it was socially expected or because they thought they could repress their natural inclinations), various forms of addiction for which the addicted person refuses to get help, and so on. Not all married people are joined together by God. Not all marriages are made in heaven.

Far too many people have been trapped in loveless or abusive marriages because of a narrow reading of Gospel passages. The message of the text is one of peace, not war; it speaks of the Christian home as the model of the love between Christ and the church. Christian marriages that do not offer this model are, perhaps, not those that need remain forever.

Building a Fence Against Violence: Turning the Other Cheek

We come now to the fifth extension, the famous case of an "eye for an eye." The version in the Sermon on the Mount begins: "You have heard that it was said, 'An eye for an eye and a tooth for a tooth'" (5:38). In the Torah, the law appears in three places: Exodus 21:23-25, Leviticus 24:19-20, and Deuteronomy 19:21. The passages spell out, in different ways, compensation for damage done to parts of the body.

This idea is cross-cultural. In Roman law, it is known as *lex talionis*, "the law of equals," or more simply as *talio* or *talion*. Rome's *Twelve Tables*, the law code traditionally dated around 451–50 BCE and inscribed on twelve tablets placed in the forum, stipulates, "If a man broke another's limb, the victim could inflict the same injury upon the wrongdoer (*talio*), but only if no settlement was agreed upon." We find similar statements in the ancient Babylonian Code of Hammurabi, but here with class distinctions: "If an *awīlu* [that is, a high-born person] should blind the eye of another *awīlu*, they shall blind his eye. . . . If he should blind the eye of a commoner or break the bone of a commoner, he shall deliver 60 shekels of silver."[3]

The Torah has no social distinctions since all bodies are in the divine image. The Torah teaching is also designed to prevent escalation of violence of the type seen in Genesis 4:24, where Lamech insists, "If Cain is avenged sevenfold, / truly Lamech seventy-sevenfold." "An eye for an eye" equalizes all bodies and limits vengeance.

Just as we have no evidence of people being stoned for adultery, we have no evidence that ancient Israelites or the Jews who came after carried out the talion. Jewish interpreters consistently deny physical mutilation as punishment for any crime. Josephus, the first-century historian writing with an eye to Gentile readers, suggests that the talion is carried out only if the victim is unwilling to accept monetary compensation: "For the law makes the sufferer the judge of the value of what he hath suffered, and permits him to estimate it, unless he will be more severe."[4] Philo, the early-first-century Jewish philosopher from Egypt, considers extenuating circumstances: whether the victim was a family member or a stranger, a ruler or a citizen, the timing of the offense, and so on.[5] The Mishnah Bava Qamma 8:1, presumes that the talion is applied only in a monetary sense: "He who injures his fellow is liable to [compensate] him on five counts: (1) injury, (2) pain, (3) medical costs, (4) loss of income, and (5) indignity."

The Babylonian Talmud Bava Qamma 84a cites, in the name of the late-first-century sage Rabbi Eliezer, that "an eye for an eye" refers to an actual eye, but this is a minority opinion. Indeed, almost all rabbinic texts suggest that the formula must mean financial compensation. They get there by logic: since no two limbs and no two eyes are equal, the destruction of one could not be compensated by the destruction of another. And, as one rabbi suggested, if a blind man took out the eye of a sighted man, what difference would it make if the blind man then lost an eye?

Jesus does not dismiss an "eye for an eye," and perhaps he, too, would have interpreted the injury in terms of monetary compensation. Jesus does *not* say, "You lost your eye; don't worry about it." He does *not* say, "You lost your eye, give to the perpetrator the other." To the contrary, he uses the talion to make a point about how to respond not to physical injury but to humiliation. Otherwise put: he changes the subject. The talion concerns physical mutilation; Jesus speaks about public humiliation: "Do not resist an evildoer. But if anyone strikes you on the right cheek, turn the other also; and if anyone wants to sue you and take your coat, give your cloak as well; and if anyone forces you to go one mile, go also the second mile" (5:39-41). The three examples— the slap, the suit, and the subjugation—together reveal their import: do not escalate violence; do not give up your agency; shame your attacker and retain your honor.

To be struck on the right cheek presumes, were the striker right-handed, a backhanded slap (you might practice this, carefully, by attempting to slap the right cheek of a brave friend). It is the slap of dismissal and humiliation. Lamentations 3:30 speaks of giving "one's cheek to the smiter, / and be filled with insults" (the Hebrew *cherpah* for "insults," connotes connotation of reproach, disgrace, scorn, and shame). In 2 Corinthians 11:20, Paul speaks about the humiliation of being slapped in the face.

To respond to such a slap, the victim has a few options, none of them good. Hitting back escalates the violence, which given social inequality, can have deadly effects. But cowering does not help either; cowering keeps the unequal and unjust system in place. Jesus offers what the biblical scholar Walter Wink called the "third way": rather than escalate the violence, and rather than lose personal dignity, face the perpetrator by making the violence and so the wrongness of the situation clear. What looks like humiliation to an outsider—being slapped, stripping naked, carrying gear—becomes an opportunity of expressing agency. By offering the left cheek, the victim resists humiliation by displaying agency and courage.

From insisting on turning the right cheek in a case of a slap, Jesus raises the issue of being sued. The setting is the court: someone "wants to sue you and take your coat." Behind this concern is Exodus 22:26-27: "If you take your neighbor's cloak in pawn, you shall restore it before the sun goes down; for it may be your neighbor's only clothing to use as cover; in what else shall that person sleep? And if your neighbor cries out to me, I will listen, for I am compassionate." Again, the victim has few options, none good. To accept the verdict is to freeze that night. To avoid the court could result in arrest and an even worse situation. But to "give your cloak as well" means to enter the court and then strip off one's garment, thereby laying bare, literally, the incivility, the injustice of the situation.

Finally, going the extra mile concerns compulsion, or as the NRSV reads, "forces you to go." We see such conscription in Matthew 27:32 (compare Mark 15:21), where Roman soldiers "compel" (the same Greek term) Simon of Cyrene to carry Jesus's crossbeam. To refuse is to risk a beating. To comply is to be humiliated. The third way accepts the inevitable: carry the baggage. Yet at the end of the mile, the conscripted peasant adds: "I'll go the second." In other words: You sought to treat me as less than human. I refuse to allow you to do this—I will use my own agency to carry it further, and in the process will humiliate you.

Building a Fence Against Limiting Love: Loving the Enemy

For the final extension, Jesus begins, "You have heard that it was said, 'You shall love your neighbor and hate your enemy'" (5:43). "Love your neighbor" comes from Leviticus 19:18, "You shall not take vengeance or bear a grudge against any of your people, but you shall love your neighbor as yourself; I am the LORD." Leviticus 19:18, concerning bearing a grudge, has the same fence-building protection as the first intensification, "If you are angry with a brother or sister, you will be liable to judgment" (5:22).

For Leviticus, "neighbor" means a fellow Israelite, a point made evident by the following injunction in Leviticus 19:34, "The alien who resides with you shall be to you as the citizen among you; you shall love the alien as yourself, for you were aliens in the land of Egypt."

The Torah distinguishes between Israelites and strangers (we might think of the distinction between a citizen and a resident alien, or members of your church and visitors from another denomination), but Leviticus insists that both must be loved.

Jesus then adds a line that is not in the Torah: "You have heard that it was said," he continues, "and hate your enemy." The Torah has no such commandment, although something resembling it appears in the Dead Sea Scrolls: "He is to teach them to love everything [or everyone]. He chose and to hate everything [or everyone] He rejected" (1QS 1:3-4).

The commandment to love enemies is anticipated by other biblical verses. Proverbs 24:17 eliminates gloating over an enemy's failures: "Do not rejoice when your enemies fall, / and do not let your heart be glad when they stumble." The rationale is not to avoid adding insult to injury, but lest "the LORD will see it and be displeased / and turn away his anger from them" (Proverbs 24:18). A similar backhanded mandate appears in Proverbs 25:21-22, "If your enemies are hungry, give them bread to eat; / and if they are thirsty, give them water to drink." The rationale is not to turn enemies into friends but to frustrate them, "for you will heap coals of fire on their heads, / and the LORD will reward you"; Paul quotes this couplet in Romans 12:20. More positive regarding enemies is Jeremiah's address to the exiled community in Babylon: "Seek the welfare of the city where I have sent you into exile, and pray to the LORD on its behalf, for in its welfare you will find your welfare" (Jeremiah 29:7).

Developing the injunction that one must pray for the welfare of the conquering empire, Jesus not only rejects hating enemies but insists, "Love your enemies and pray for those who persecute you" (Matthew 5:44). The rationale: people should act as God acts "so that you may be children of your Father in heaven" who is concerned about the righteous and the unrighteous alike (5:45). To be children of the Father means acting as that Father would act. A similar teaching appears in the Babylonian Talmud: "Abba Shaul says: . . . Just as He is compassionate and merciful, so too should you be compassionate and merciful" (Shabbat 133b).

How one prays for one's enemies is another matter. *Fiddler on the Roof* offers the following exchange:

MENDEL: "Rabbi, may I ask you a question?"
RABBI: "Certainly, my son."
MENDEL: "Is there a proper blessing for the tsar?"
RABBI: "A blessing for the tsar? Of course! May God bless and keep the tsar . . . far away from us!"[6]

If we prayed for our enemies, perhaps we would be less likely, internationally, to drop bombs or, locally, to spread gossip.

To love our enemies as ourselves—which first requires that we, in fact, love ourselves (a point that cannot be taken for granted)—is not easy. It means praying not only for the rival team or the obnoxious boss but also for the neo-Nazi and the KKK member. They, too, are in God's image and likeness, no matter how deformed that image has become. God forbid that we would descend into that same deformity by rejoicing in the sufferings of others, even those whom we would call the enemy.

Upkeep on the Fence

Jesus's remarks are not antitheses, and he does not reject the Scriptures of Israel in favor of a new law. Once we know the ancient context of these teachings, we are better able to determine how they should be presented in today's contexts.

A 2014 Gallup poll reported, "Americans who favor the death penalty most often cite 'an eye for an eye' as the reason they hold their position."[7] In Jesus's citation of the talion, he does not mention "a life for a life." Thus, the claim that Jesus would approve of capital punishment receives support only from what is *not* said.

Justice without mercy—an "eye for an eye" taken literally—is intolerable. Yet mercy without justice—as in a permanent physical injury that receives no compensation at all or receives unequal compensation based on the economic status of the perpetrator—is equally intolerable. The Sermon on the Mount forces us to reflect on both justice and mercy; ideally, through reflection comes wisdom.

Chapter 3

PRACTICING PIETY

The earliest copies of the New Testament that we have lack chapter and verse divisions, and there is no reason to think that an ancient evangelist telling Matthew's story of Jesus to an audience of men and women, children and adults, slaves and free, Jews and pagans would have stopped at the end of chapter 5. Therefore, as we begin Matthew 6, a chapter that includes the Our Father prayer, we hear several echoes of chapter 5. The opening of chapter 6 concerns how disciples are to practice their piety, and suddenly it occurs to us: the Beatitudes and the extensions are all about the practice of piety. To be a disciple means less about believing in a set of propositions and more about acting upon God's Word as interpreted by Jesus. As we hear those echoes, we realize that the Sermon on the Mount is designed to encourage us to recognize the potential we have, as created in the image and likeness of God, to act as if divine will occurs on earth as it does in heaven.

To appreciate the beginning of Matthew 6, we shall therefore backtrack briefly to Matthew 5 and recover a few of the verses that are not part of either the Beatitudes or the extensions. These verses set the scene for how piety—our expressions of our religious commitments—should be practiced.

"You are the salt of the earth"

The expression "salt of the earth" has become, like the Beatitudes and the extensions, a cliché. It's the title of a 2015 documentary film about the Brazilian photographer Sebastião Salgado;

it's the final cut, written by Mick Jagger and Keith Richards and accompanied by the Los Angeles Watts Street Gospel Choir, on the 1968 Rolling Stones album *Beggars Banquet*. As splendid as the documentary is, and as classic as the song is, the original statement offers more.

"You are the salt of the earth" is not a command but a fact; Jesus identifies his disciples (that "you" is plural) as salt. So far so good; we can immediately come up with explanations for the metaphor: salt is a preservative; salt is a seasoning; salt is needed for life; salt is needed for the manufacture of toothpaste, bath soap, bleaches, and dyes; salt is needed for the treatment of icy roads and carpet stains, and a host of other things. Any of these applications, and more, can find a home in the interpretation of Matthew 5:13, including multiple meanings that may never have occurred to Jesus's first disciples or Matthew's first readers.

Some of us will recall one or more of the Bible's other references to salt. There's Mrs. Lot, who is turned into a pillar of salt because she looked back at her burning home in Sodom (Genesis 19:26). When I was little, I thought she was turned into a pillow of salt, like the desiccation pillows packed inside shoeboxes and some medications. Whether a pillar of salt or a pillow of salt, neither strikes me as appetizing. That negative exemplar continues in the New Testament's single reference to Mrs. Lot. In Luke 17:32, Jesus enigmatically states, "Remember Lot's wife." The point there is not to look back—to self-sufficiency, to personal rather than communal relations, to stuff, to the realm of sin—when heading on the path of the kingdom, for as the next line in Luke states, "Those who try to make their life secure will lose it, but those who lose their life will keep it." Though the reference to salt in the Sermon on the Mount reminds me of Mrs. Lot, I don't think she is the reference to "salt of the earth."

Staying in the Bible, we might think of the salt used for sacrifices; Exodus 30:35, for example, speaks of an "incense blended as by the perfumer, seasoned with salt, pure and holy." We might recall cities sown with salt so that nothing will grow in their fields (for example, Judges 9:45). Sirach, otherwise known as Ecclesiasticus, a canonical book in the Roman Catholic, Anglican, and Eastern Orthodox communions, states that "sand, salt, and a piece of iron / are easier to bear than a stupid person" (Sirach 22:15). Any of these references can bring meaning to Jesus's statement. Again, not all salt references may be relevant to our verse in Matthew 6. We can do better.

First, to get at the heart of the statement, we need to address the reference not only to salt but also to the earth: you are the salt *of the earth*. The disciples do not exist to show off their taste or color; they exist not for themselves but for the world. The disciples are to season, to color, to make more alive *the world*. Their very presence is a blessing. When any person sees them, that person can take heart in knowing that the disciples represent what is good in the world.

Second, they represent what is valuable. The word *salt* comes from the Latin *sel*, which is also the origin of the English word *salary*; the monthly payment to Roman soldiers, called *salarium*, was in salt. Today salt is ever-present and, given oversalted food, often too present. At the time of Jesus, it was both a precious commodity and the payment that kept the army moving. For the disciples to be the salt of the earth, they necessarily have value; they make the heavenly host manifest on earth.

Third, for all its value, salt is also a simple element. Salt does not have to be enhanced by something else; salt is rather the enhancer. That simple aspect does not mean that disciples, as the "salt of the earth," are undereducated; to the contrary, they are the ones who have studied their own tradition and interpreted it in light of Jesus's teachings. In turn, they themselves teach, and live, the gospel not in an ostentatious way and not with the need for the obscurity that sometimes finds its way into theological discourse.

Fourth, just as we cannot live with too little salt, we also cannot live with *too much* salt. Salt loses its saltiness when it becomes diluted with various things—such as the cares of the world (see Matthew 13:22)—and then it has no value. Too much salt is worse.

Too much salt says, "Look at me," and that approach, literally, is deadly to faith. Oversalted pastors in the pulpit give sermons that point to themselves rather than to the Scripture; oversalted disciples seek to be rewarded for good works on earth rather than works that give glory to God. But those disciples who are the salt of the earth have gotten past the egotistic mode that says, "Look at me"; they are poor in spirit, meek, and merciful. The best salt—in food, in medicine, in dyes—is almost undetected. It does its work *not* by calling attention to itself but by brightening, making more alive, everything it permeates.

From these four points, it is easy to see how the disciples are the salt of the earth. On the local level, to be the salt of the earth means to participate in what we conventionally call random acts of kindness, even just making eye contact or smiling at someone. Those simple gestures, repeated across the globe, change moods; they literally brighten our days and serve to heal wounded souls.

Next, to be the salt of the earth means to be true to oneself. The disciple does not have to think about being salt; the disciple is salt. I realize that sounds a tad weird, as if one is saying, "You're a chair," or, "You're a hot pepper." The idea comes from the Beatitudes: just as the disciples know that they are already blessed, already loved, already part of a new family of faith, they also know that their nature has changed. They are not pieces of dust; they are not specks of dirt. They are salt. They do not just *have* motivation; they *are* motivation.

Finally, disciples who can recognize their role as the salt of the earth recognize that they are valuable not simply because of who they are but also and especially for what they contribute to the world.

"You are the light of the world"

"You are the salt of the earth" finds a parallel in Jesus's next statement, "You are the light of the world." Again, we can play with the metaphor: we need light for plants to grow (most of us can remember learning about, and having difficulty spelling, *photosynthesis*), for an ecologically friendly power source (for example, solar panels), for seeing more clearly, and so on. We can think of various sources of light: the sun, stars, fire. And we can find numerous examples of light imagery in the Bible, starting as early as Genesis 1:3, "Then God said, 'Let there be light'; and there was light." Psalm 119:105 famously proclaims, "Your word is a lamp to my feet / and a light to my path." The last chapter in the Christian Bible, Revelation 22, returns to Genesis in claiming that in that final heavenly Jerusalem, "there will be no more night; they need no light of lamp or sun, for the Lord God will be their light, and they will reign forever and ever" (v. 5). There are well over two hundred more references to light in the Bible, and all can, well, shed some light on our verse in Matthew.

But, we can focus more precisely. For example, just as salt is necessary for life, so is light. Without light, we have no plants, no warmth, no beacons. Next, just as salt can become so diluted that it loses its intrinsic character as salt, so darkness, as the Gospel of John puts it, seeks to overcome the light (John 1:5). "This little light of mine" can shine, but it can also be snuffed out. Thus light, too, is a precious commodity that must be preserved. And just as too much salt can kill, too much light can blind. Effective light does not call attention to itself; rather, it lights up the world.

Compared to salt, however, light has greater theological implications. In the Sermon on the Mount, Jesus tells his disciples, "*You are* the light of the world"; in John's Gospel, he tells his disciples, "*I am* the light of the world. Whoever follows me will never walk in darkness but will have the light of life" (John 8:12, italics added; compare 11:9). The Sermon on the Mount and the Gospel of John complement each other.

For the disciples, Jesus is the light of the world. Yet as he states in John 9:5, he is the light "as long as I am in the world." The disciples therefore take up his role: acting as he instructs them and, as we see in Matthew, as he himself acts, they too can be the light of the world. More, he is in the world when his disciples recognize his presence in others: "For I was hungry and you gave me food, I was thirsty and you gave me something to drink, I was a stranger and you welcomed me, I was naked and you gave me clothing, I was sick and you took care of me, I was in prison and you visited me" (Matthew 25:35-36).

Once the disciples recognize that they are light, they also recognize that their role is to shine so that others can find their way. Jesus knows that, just as salt can lose its intrinsic identity, light can be hoarded and fail to fulfill its proper function. He states first the obvious: "A city built on a hill cannot be hid" (Matthew 5:14). His followers are to become like that city: a refuge, a home, a place where there is salt and light, love and compassion.

He next extends the obvious point: "No one after lighting a lamp puts it under the bushel basket, but on the lampstand, and it gives light to all in the house" (Matthew 5:15). The house is where the disciples gather; Peter's house becomes a site of healing; the home of Mary and Martha (Luke 10:38-42; compare John 11–12) becomes a refuge for Jesus; the home of Mary the mother of John Mark hosts the followers in the early post-Easter years in Jerusalem (Acts 12:12). Paul set up what we call "house churches" for his Gentile converts.

That light cannot be restricted to the house church (or any church building or community), as the city metaphor indicates. To be the light of the world is to shine not only in the dark places of prisons and soup kitchens but also in any place where there is loneliness or despair, sickness or pain. Even in times and places, still today, when the church has had literally to go underground, it cannot be hid since it is known for its good deeds. Jesus knows this; he had already assured his disciples, "Blessed are you when people revile you and persecute you and utter all kinds of evil against you falsely on my account" (Matthew 5:11).

If we think of a church as a house, as a home where family and friends gather, we get a different image than if we think of a place to be visited maybe for an hour on Sunday. And if we think of our homes as the place where our light shines, we are more likely to be patient with the children or with those whose minds have reverted to childhood; we are more likely to find that light within ourselves as we go through the day.

The section concludes by noting that the salt and the light do not point to themselves: "In the same way, let your light shine before others, so that they may see your good works and give glory to your Father in heaven" (Matthew 5:16). This comment makes a number of my students nervous: "That's works righteousness," they suggest. "We are not saved by works, but by grace." Even the idea of practicing piety disturbs them. It shouldn't.

Any faith that does not manifest itself in works is not faith; it is complacency and self-satisfaction. It is not salt, because it contributes nothing to the earth. It is not light, since its shining is only for self-reflection. Disciples are to glorify God by being their true selves: salt and light; existing for others rather than for only themselves and doing works prompt others to do the same. The action of the disciple should be light and salt to the earth and the world, not just to those inside their own house.

As we move into Matthew 6, on practicing piety, disciples take with them the metaphors of salt and light, and they know in each case that the focus is not on them but on what they do, how they impact others, and the seasoning and the guiding they provide.

Be Perfect; Don't Panic

At the end of Matthew 5, Jesus states,

> You have heard that it was said, "You shall love your neighbor and hate your enemy." But I say to you, Love your enemies and pray for those who persecute you, so that you may be children of your Father in heaven; for he makes his sun rise on the evil and on the good, and sends rain on the righteous

and on the unrighteous. . . . Be perfect, therefore, as your
heavenly Father is perfect. (vv. 43-45, 48)

He asks a lot. We can pray for our enemies; it's relatively easy
to do in the sanctuary of, well, a sanctuary. In fact, such prayers
can make us feel quite good about ourselves. He's asking for more.

My mother took the next step: she told me always to be un-
failingly nice, even to people who are nasty. "You should always be
a lady," she told me (that sounds so 1960s); "don't stoop to their
level." That was also asking for a lot. But it could be done, and I
admit to feeling pretty good about not repaying nastiness with more
nastiness. Yet I still had that sense of self-satisfaction: "I'm better
than they are. And I got higher grades as well."

Jesus is still asking for more.

He instructs: act the way God would act; act as if you fully recognized that your enemy is also in the image and likeness of God.

The NRSV reads, "Be perfect," as if Jesus is issuing a command. Not quite. While that "you" is in a place of prominence and
while the verb can function as an imperative, the Greek verb is not
an imperative but a future indicative. Jesus states that if we follow
his instructions, we "will be perfect." He is less giving a command
than making a statement. This teaching is no more and no less audacious than the Torah's teaching, "You shall be holy, for I the LORD
your God am holy" (Leviticus 19:2; compare 1 Peter 1:16).

The point is not that we are to *be* God but that God sets the
standard for us. We are but a little lower than God (so Psalm 8:5;
the Septuagint, finding that verse too audacious, rewrote to say that
mortals are but a little lower than the *angels*). God sets a high standard for us; there is no better standard. At the same time, Jesus
asks nothing of his disciples that he does not ask of himself.

Finally, as always, we should be wary of translations. The Greek
term the NRSV translates as "be perfect" is *teleios*, a form of the
word *telos*, meaning "complete." (Anyone who has taken a theology
or philosophy course is likely to be familiar with the term *teleology*,
matters concerning purpose, whether of things or people or the

world). In the Bible, the term rarely has the primary connotation of "perfect" in the sense of "never doing anything wrong or incomplete." Nor is Jesus calling us to a type of perfectionism that would necessarily make us all neurotic.

The term is probably best translated not "perfect" but "complete," as we see in the NRSV's reading of James 1:4, "Let endurance have its full effect, so that you may be mature and complete [*teleios*], lacking in nothing." In fact, the Epistle of James is the best intertext for the Sermon the Mount since it frequently repeats Jesus's sayings found in Matthew 5–7. James goes on to note—after advising that "not many of you should become teachers . . . for you know that we who teach will be judged with greater strictness" (I should have paid more attention to *that* verse)—that "all of us make many mistakes. Anyone who makes no mistakes in speaking is perfect" (James 3:1-2). James is not saying that making mistakes is OK; to the contrary, he admits that we need to keep working on ourselves, and we need to keep helping our neighbors since we are not (yet) perfect.

To be perfect, or complete, is thus a goal, and because it is a goal, it is necessarily part of a process. We may never get there, at least in this life. And that's OK, as long as we persevere, as long as disciples keep their basic essence as salt and light. King Solomon, upon dedicating the Temple in Jerusalem, proclaimed to the people, "Therefore devote yourselves completely to the LORD our God, walking in his statutes and keeping his commandments, as at this day" (1 Kings 8:61). The Septuagint uses *teleios* for the term translated by the NRSV as "completely." And the original Hebrew reads *shalem*, "whole" or "complete"; the word is a cognate of the more familiar Hebrew term *shalom*, "peace."

This linguistic exercise leads to both a challenge and a comfort. The disciples are already blessed; they are already salt and light; they have the best model possible for continuing on the path to the kingdom of heaven; they are moving toward being complete and at peace.

When I would bring home a paper with a grade of 100, my mother would smile at me and ask, "You couldn't have gotten a 101?" We are on our way, but we can always do better.

Beware of Practicing—to Be Seen

Matthew 6 begins, "Beware of practicing your piety before others in order to be seen by them." The Greek term the NRSV translates as "piety" is *dikaiosynē,* a term usually translated as "righteousness" or "justice." Matthew uses the term several times in the Sermon on the Mount and elsewhere in the Gospel, and those other uses give us clues as to what it means here.

The first use is Matthew 3:15, where Jesus meets John the Baptist. John thinks that Jesus, being the Messiah, should baptize him, but Jesus insists that John perform the ritual: "Let it be so now; for it is proper for us in this way to fulfill all righteousness [*dikaiosynē*]." The point, brought to light in Matthew 6:1, is that righteousness should never be displayed for personal aggrandizement. Although he is Lord, Jesus insists on taking the position of any other human being.

With that same sense of concern for others rather than self-promotion, Jesus includes *dikaiosynē* in the Beatitudes: "Blessed are those who hunger and thirst for righteousness [*dikaiosynē*], for they will be filled" (Matthew 5:6). Given the stress the Beatitudes place on humility, interdependence, not lording it over others, the term here again takes the focus off the individual and places it where it belongs. *Dikaiosynē* reappears in 5:10, another Beatitude: "Blessed are those who are persecuted for righteousness' [*dikaiosynē*] sake, for theirs is the kingdom of heaven."

Twice more the term appears in the Sermon on the Mount. In Matthew 5:20, Jesus tells his disciples, "Unless your righteousness exceeds that of the scribes and Pharisees, you will never enter the kingdom of heaven." He is, again, setting a high bar. The disciples have to be more righteous than those who were, in the popular view, both talking the talk *and walking the walk*. According to Josephus, who was no fan of the Pharisees, "They live [simply], and despise delicacies in diet; and they follow the conduct of reason; and what that prescribes to them as good for them they do; and they think they ought earnestly to strive to observe reason's dictates for practice. They also pay a respect to such as are in years; nor are they so bold as to contradict them in any thing which they have introduced."[1] He also states that "Pharisees are friendly to one another, and are for the exercise of concord, and regard for the public."[2] Even Paul celebrates his Pharisaic connections (Philippians 3:5).

Finally, toward the end of Matthew 6, Jesus states, "But strive first for the kingdom of God and his righteousness [yes, *dikaiosynē*], and all these things will be given to you as well." To be righteous, to practice the correct type of piety, is to have one foot in the kingdom of heaven.

The verse puts us in a quandary: good acts, acts of righteousness and justice, have to have a public impact since, as salt and light, the disciples necessarily relate to the lives of others. How then do disciples avoid practicing their piety before others? The answer is simple: if the practice is based in justice, that's fine; if it's based on self-interest, "in order to be seen by" others, then it is not. As he did with the extensions, Jesus is looking not only at the action but also at the motive behind it. When motive and action work in harmony, when the head is aligned with the heart, then we are moving toward that goal of "completion" or "perfection."

Giving Alms

Jesus then gives a perfect example of the wrong type of piety, of piety practiced so that it will be seen by others: charitable giving. He is not saying do not give to charity; rather, he is suggesting how best such donations should be made.

In Jewish tradition, supporting the poor is a central commandment; Deuteronomy 15:11 mandates, "Since there will never cease to be some in need on the earth, I therefore command you, 'Open your hand to the poor and needy neighbor in your land.'" Care for the poor is so central that the Hebrew terms for "righteousness" and "almsgiving" come from the same root, as if to echo: the one who gives support to others (Hebrew: *tzadik*) is righteous (*tzedakah*). Making this linguistic connection even more profound: the Hebrew term for "righteousness," *tzedakah*, comes into Greek as *dikaiosynē*, which we just discussed.

The problem: making donations is a perfect opportunity for publicizing magnanimity. Therefore, Jesus instructs, "Whenever you give alms, do not sound a trumpet before you, as the hypocrites do in the synagogues and in the streets, so that they may be praised by others. Truly [Greek and Hebrew: *amen*] I tell you, they have received their reward" (Matthew 6:2). This requires unpacking.

The reference to trumpet-sounding is a figure of speech. Folks in the first century were not walking around with a trumpet or a shofar (a ram's horn) or a saxophone and tooting every time someone donated a shekel. But then, as well as now, it is likely that major donors were known. Acts 4:36-37, for example, mentions a fellow named Joseph, a Levite (Jewish priest) from Cyprus, who "sold a field that belonged to him, then brought the money, and laid it at the apostles' feet." Nicknamed Barnabas (Aramaic for "son of encouragement"), he will become Paul's coevangelist.

We have similar shout-outs today, whether in lists of donors for a charitable event or names on classrooms or buildings or endowed chairs. There is nothing wrong with generosity, and there is nothing wrong with thanking people for it. And yet . . .

Jesus raises several questions worth considering: Do we want our names on the buildings, and if so, why? To honor ourselves? To show our commitments so that our children and our children's children will know them? Do we make donations in our own names, or do we contribute to honor or memorialize others (for example, a scholarship in the name of my mother and father)?

How are we to give? Jesus suggests, "But when you give alms, do not let your left hand know what your right hand is doing, so that your alms may be done in secret; and your Father who sees in secret will reward you" (Matthew 6:3-4). We do not need, and should not even desire, public recognition; nothing could be greater, of more value, than God responding, "Well done."

The great Jewish teacher Maimonides (1138–1204), spoke of eight levels of charity, and his comments fit neatly with Jesus's advice.

The lowest level is giving unwillingly. Many of us have been there: responding to the friend who asks that we contribute to *her* favorite charity; the person on the street who looks sufficiently pathetic that we turn over a few dollars. The good news is that charity is given; the bad news: we don't feel very good about the process.

The second level is to give willingly but inadequately. Most of us can happily put a dollar in a collection plate. We could give more. But if we remain happy with the lesser amount, we are not as close to the kingdom as we might be. Here we might recall the story of the widow's mite (alas, it appears in Mark and Luke but not in Matthew). This is Mark 12:41-44:

> [Jesus] sat down opposite the treasury, and watched the crowd putting money into the treasury. Many rich people put in large sums. A poor widow came and put in two small copper coins, which are worth a penny. Then he called his disciples and said to them, "Truly I tell you, this poor widow has put in more than all those who are contributing to the treasury. For all of them have contributed out of their abundance; but she out of her poverty has put in everything she had, all she had to live on."

Jesus's focus, appropriately, is on quality not quantity.

The third level is to give only after being asked. Since the poor will always be with us, as Deuteronomy states and as Jesus repeats (see Matthew 26:11), we should always set aside something for those who have less than we do. We should not need to be asked. When I was a child, we had in our house a *pushke* (a Yiddish term), a small box with a slit on the top. Every Friday night my father would put whatever change he had in his pocket (after letting me check the dates on the pennies for my penny collection) into the *pushke*. When it was full, we would bring it to the rabbi, who put the money in his discretionary fund to help poorer members of the synagogue. We did not need to be asked; the practice was presumed. (Personally, I thought this a better option than the piggy bank my friends had; the piggy bank somehow seemed unkosher to me.)

Fourth is giving to the poor *before* the request comes. We see the poverty in front of us, and we write the check. Nothing wrong here, save that we wait until the problem of poverty confronts us. Even better would be to contribute before poverty hits us in the face.

Fifth is when we give anonymously, but the beneficiary knows our identity. Maimonides speaks of how the sages would attach coins to their robes, so that the poor could take them out without the humiliation of having to receive charity directly. This strikes me as awkward; why tie coins to your robes, or stick bills in your pocket, so that people can come take the coins? There should be a better delivery form.

Sixth is when the benefactor knows the recipient, but the recipient does not know the benefactor. The problem here is the pity that the benefactor feels. More, the recipients have no chance of expressing appreciation, which puts them in an awkward situation.

Seventh is the approach Jesus suggests: benefactor and recipient do not know each other's identity. The Jerusalem Temple had such a system: the righteous would contribute what they could, and the poor would take what they needed. No one felt ashamed. This system also helps those who can no longer maintain their current status: the breadwinner who, after thirty years at the same company, is declared redundant; the family overwhelmed with medical bills and insufficient insurance; the next-door neighbor who, unknown to all, is faced with either feeding the family or paying the electric bill.

Maimonides offers one more level: offer a financial base or enter into partnership so that the person in poverty will no longer require charity but will become financially secure. This is the teaching behind the more familiar saying—the origins of which may be with Maimonides himself—"Give a man a fish, and you feed him for a day. Teach a man to fish, and you feed him for a lifetime." Jesus calls to his disciples, "Follow me, and I will make you fish for people" (Matthew 4:19). I'd like to think that this fishing also included lessons on how those people might themselves take up metaphoric fishing and so welcome others into their circle.

In all cases, charitable giving, "righteousness" or "piety," requires a concern for dignity. It is the same dignity that Jesus has in mind when he speaks about refusing to respond to violence with more violence, even if one is slapped, sued, or commandeered.

At the same time, the focus on charitable giving reminds all of us of two facts. First, the one who is generous today may be in a position of need tomorrow. When we give to help others, we should realize not a sense of pride but a sense of humility, since it makes manifest the fragility of life. Second, everyone has something to give, whether it be time or funding or resources. To be a Jew, and by extension to be a member of the family of Jesus, means to be in community—or better, in a family—where concerns are voiced, needs are met, and everyone pitches in to help.

Jesus ends this discussion with the notice that after the disciples make their donation in secret, "your Father who sees in secret will reward you" (Matthew 6:4). This is another verse that makes some of my students nervous, as it suggests that dreaded "works righteousness." Such nervousness is easily alleviated. First, the giving is not designed *so that* one gets a reward. The giving is done because we, in the image and likeness of God, act generously as God acts. Second, the sense of reward here should be seen in the context of the Beatitudes: the meek (who would never trumpet their generosity) will inherit the earth (Matthew 5:5); those who hunger and thirst for righteousness (who would necessarily act righteously, or piously, toward others) will be filled (Matthew 5:6). God approves of our actions, especially when they are done because we have taken to heart the commandment to love our neighbors as ourselves.

We might attend to the particulars of the address. The Beatitudes are in the plural: those who are "poor in spirit" are all the disciples from those sitting with Jesus to baptized people today. When Jesus tells them, "You are the salt of the earth" (Matthew 5:13), that "you" is also in the plural. But when he speaks about giving alms in Matthew 6:2, he shifts to the singular. It is the "you all" of the community who are the salt of the earth and the light of the world. When its members step into the kingdom of heaven, the church—the body of the Christ on earth—is glorified. Nothing wrong with that!

And When You Pray . . .

All conversations with God are a form of prayer. Prayer can praise; it can lament or demand or accuse. Prayer suggests relationship: regardless of how angry we may be at God—and we have lots of reasons to be angry, from the death of a loved one to global issues such as war, poverty, genocide, and natural destruction—prayer says that we are still connected. Prayer means that the channels are still open and that we have not walked away from either personal or community-defined piety.

Prayer in anger is *not* hypocrisy; it is honesty. Prayer that asks "why" is *not* a sign of disbelief; it expresses our human resistance to chaos. Prayer *should* ask why, and the Bible gives us examples. Psalm 22 begins, "My God, my God, why have you forsaken me? / Why are you so far from helping me, from the words of my groaning?" Psalm 42:9 asks,

> I say to God, my rock,
> "Why have you forgotten me?
> Why must I walk about mournfully
> because the enemy oppresses me?"

Even prayer that asks for the destruction of the enemy is of value. Isaiah 13:16 states, regarding the Babylonians who conquered Judea and destroyed Solomon's Temple:

> Their infants will be dashed to pieces
>> before their eyes;
> their houses will be plundered,
>> and their wives ravished.

The verse is horrible; it is also brutally honesty. I appreciate this honesty. It states how the victims felt; it allows them to cry out their despair.

And then . . . Once we recite the words, we recognize how horrible the wish is. We realize the violence of which we are capable, and we pull back. Jesus reminds us, "But I say to you, Love your enemies and pray for those who persecute you" (Matthew 5:44). The effect of putting Isaiah's horrific statement alongside Jesus's instruction is exactly what it should be: we recognize the violence of which we—of which anyone—are capable, and then we recognize that we should not act like our enemies. To the contrary.

Next, prayer should be focused on God, not on the one offering the prayer. Therefore Jesus instructs, "And whenever you pray, do not be like the hypocrites; for they love to stand and pray in the synagogues and at the street corners, so that they may be seen by others. Truly I tell you, they have received their reward" (Matthew 6:5).

The expression "received their reward" appears three times in the Sermon on the Mount, and in each case it has the same implication: show off on earth and you do not need a heavenly recognition. Regarding almsgiving, Jesus warns: don't make a show of your charity donations; that may get you earthly glory but not heavenly recognition (Matthew 6:2). Now, in relation to prayer, he insists, don't make a public spectacle of yourselves—whether in a house of worship or in public—"so that [you] may be seen by others."

This concern for showing off appears once more in the Sermon on the Mount, right after the Our Father prayer. Continuing the topic of piety, Jesus mandates, "Whenever you fast, do not look dismal, like the hypocrites, for they disfigure their faces so as to show others that they are fasting. Truly I tell you, they have received their reward" (Matthew 6:16).

Showing off in prayer is nothing new, despite the fact that it is annoying to pretty much everyone except the showoff. The grace before meals at public events that goes on for fifteen minutes may be the most common example. This may be one of the reasons why the traditional Jewish blessing before a meal—"Blessed are You, Lord, our God, ruler of the universe, who brings forth bread from the earth"—is so short, and the prayer after the meal is much, much longer. That also makes sense to me: it is more effective to offer thanks after we have enjoyed that for which we are giving thanks.

Jesus particularly speaks against the tendency to "heap up empty phrases" or the belief that "many words" will catch God's ear (Matthew 6:7). God already knows what we want; the prayer is our opportunity to put those needs into words. We don't need five pages when five words will do.

One of my favorite Jewish stories is that of a little boy who comes to the synagogue and recites, over and over, the first three letters of the Hebrew alphabet: *aleph, bet, gimel* (those of you who know the Greek alphabet should see similarities to *alpha, beta, gamma*). Smiling, the rabbi asks the child, "What are you doing?" The little boy responds, "I don't know the prayers and I can't read, but if I just say the letters, God puts the prayer together for me." The first three letters of the alphabet are all we need. We do not need the perfect words, and we do not need to go on for five or ten or (God forbid) twenty minutes.

If we can't find the right words, it doesn't matter. We can always use the Psalms as a prompt or just remain silently in prayer: God can put the thoughts together.

Public prayer is sometimes necessary. The Kaddish, recited by those in mourning, can only be recited in a quorum of ten other Jews. The tradition also means that those in mourning are never alone. To this day, most synagogues will have a service every morning and every evening so that those in mourning—or those commemorating the anniversary of a person's death (the *yahrzeit*), which we discussed in relation to Jesus's comment "blessed are those who mourn" (Matthew 5:4)—know that they are not alone. Individuals die; the community lives, and it comforts.

For personal prayer, Jesus advises, "Go into your room and shut the door and pray to your Father who is in secret; and your Father who sees in secret will reward you" (6:6). He is *not* saying keep your concerns to yourself. He is *not* saying avoid any type of public activity that might be associated with faith. And he is *not* saying stop all prayer in the synagogue (and so, by extension, the church). He rather speaks of those private prayers that, if said publicly, can give the impression of "acting religious" and so calling attention to the one praying rather than to God.

From avoiding practicing piety in order to show off, Jesus turns to practicing piety with the goal of manipulating God. He takes his cue from what he perceives to be non-Jewish practice: "'When you are praying, do not heap up empty phrases as the Gentiles do; for they think that they will be heard because of their many words. Do not be like them, for your Father knows what you need before you ask him'" (6:7-8). Heaping up terms suggests that if we pray long enough or hit the right notes then God—operating on automatic—will grant us what we want. Heaping up phrases in prayer reminds me of students who write for quantity of words rather than quality of discussion. God is not your professor (and your professor is not God), although neither finds substituting quantity for quality helpful. We need not butter God up or bang on God's door.

Finally, we don't have to worry about bothering God with personal concerns. In the temple at Shiloh, Hannah—suffering not only from infertility but also from the taunts of her fertile cowife Peninnah—begs God for a child. "She was deeply distressed and prayed to the LORD, and wept bitterly. . . . As she continued praying before the LORD, Eli [the priest] observed her mouth. Hannah was praying silently; only her lips moved, but her voice was not heard; therefore Eli thought she was drunk" (1 Samuel 1:10, 12-13). She asks for what she wanted, honestly and passionately. From Hannah's prayer comes the Jewish tradition that when we pray, no matter if we know the prayer by heart, we do not merely read the words with our eyes but also say the words with our lips. That practice helps us better focus on the words, even as we come to know that prayer is a matter not only of the heart but also of the body.

Jesus prays, frequently. In Matthew, he prays after the feeding of the five thousand (or, better, twenty-five thousand, since Matthew says the five thousand are "besides women and children" [Matthew 14:21]) and immediately before he walks on water. The miracles may exhaust him. Still, he has to teach his followers that, despite his powers, his true role lies not in miracle or power; rather, "just as the Son of Man came not to be served but to serve, and to give his life a ransom for many" (20:28). He prays in Gethsemane, three times, "My Father, if it is possible, let this cup pass from me; yet not what I want but what you want" (26:39; compare 26:41; 26:44), and he tells his disciples that they should "Stay awake and pray that [they] may not come into the time of trial" (26:41). "Do not come into the time of trial" could also be translated "Do not bring us into temptation," and that line leads us to our next chapter on the Our Father prayer.

Chapter 4

OUR FATHER

When I was in the first grade at Job S. Gidley Elementary School in North Dartmouth, Massachusetts, Mrs. Cross (appropriately named, for the symbolism not for the attitude) led the class in reciting the Pledge of Allegiance, "The Star-Spangled Banner," and the Our Father. For the prayer, we sat at our desks, folded our hands, and bowed our heads. So after pledging loyalty to "liver tea" and singing about the "donnzerly" light, I'm sure I was not the only one in the class who bowed my head and prayed, "Our Father, who art in heaven, Harold be thy name. . . . Lead us not into Penn Station . . ." Then again, I thought the name of the school was "job" as in "get a job" and not "Job" as in the book. Little children have much to learn.

If we get the words of the prayer wrong, we may find some meaning nevertheless; after all, Penn Station was a very crowded place, and the one time I had been there, my mother held my hand very tightly. But if we attend to the correct words, and then we set them in their historical context—as a prayer one Jew teaches his fellow Jews—we find words that are not only comprehensible regardless of location but also profound.

"Pray then in this way"

In the previous verses, Jesus instructs his disciples on prayer, instructions that still hold for today. First, do not be ostentatious in prayer (Matthew 6:1); the focus of prayer should always be on God, not the clergy, not the choir, not the congregant.

Second, do not deliberately stake out a place where people can see you (6:5). For those times when you want to pray and you are not at that moment participating in a worship service, speak to God in private (6:6). Jesus is not eliminating communal prayer; he himself engages in synagogue worship, and his Jewish followers worshipped in both synagogues and the Jerusalem Temple, as we see in the Book of Acts. He is rather using this image of secret prayer to make the point about how we pray, especially in a public setting.

A private prayer may of course be said during a worship service, and many churches provide moments of personal prayer and reflection as part of the liturgy. These are, depending on denomination, called "prayers of the people," "prayers of the congregation," "joys and concerns," and so on.

In synagogues, it is increasingly common for the congregation to pray a Mi Sheberach (pronounced *mee sh'bay-rakh*), literally, "May the one who blessed." As the Our Father neatly demonstrates, Jewish prayers are typically named for their first words. The Mi Sheberach, traditionally recited at a service when the Torah is read, such as a Sabbath service, is a short prayer for healing: "May the One Who blessed our ancestors, Abraham, Isaac, and Jacob, Sarah, Rebecca, Rachel, and Leah, bless and heal those who are ill [at this point, the members of the congregation recite the names of their relatives and friends who are ill]. May the Blessed Holy One be filled with compassion for their health to be restored and their strength to be revived. May God swiftly send them a complete renewal of body and spirit, and let us say 'Amen.'" The prayer provides comfort to the friends and relatives; at the same time, because it is public, it serves as a way of alerting members of the congregation to who is ailing and who might need support.

Finally, Jesus advises that the disciples not "heap up empty phrases" since God does not need "many words" (6:7). God already knows what we want because God is aware of what is in our hearts.

The purpose of prayer is not to get God's attention. We already have God's attention. Prayer serves other functions; here are just five. First, it allows us to express, honestly, our feelings: of worry and anger, thanksgiving and celebration. The Psalms, which express all of these concerns and more, provide us numerous guidelines. In turn, studying the Psalms—and in Judaism, study of the Scriptures and the commentaries on them *is* a form of worship—helps us pray, as it provides us words we might not have considered or prompts us to give thanks for insights we might not otherwise have had.

Second, prayer—like any form of communication—can improve a relationship. Ideally, the more we talk with our parents, our partners, or our children, the more we understand them, and the more they understand us. The more we pray, the better we can develop our relationship with the divine. For some, prayer is as much a part of the daily routine as brushing one's teeth (both are healthy activities). Deuteronomy 6, which includes the famous "Hear O Israel: the LORD is Our God, the LORD alone" (v. 4) and "You shall love the LORD your God with all your heart, and with all your soul, and with all your might" (v. 5), goes on to state about the Torah, "Recite [these words] to your children and talk about them when you are at home and when you are away, when you lie down and when you rise" (v. 7); thus, traditional Jews have morning and evening prayers as well as prayers said with the congregation.

This familial model also helps us with understanding Paul's comment in 1 Thessalonians 5:17, "Pray without ceasing." I've heard from a number of people—especially those who are new to Christian belief—worried that they sometimes *don't* pray; they find themselves thinking of matters other than prayer, and so they worry that they have fallen into sin, failed Jesus, or otherwise insufficiently practiced their faith. They have misread Paul. The apostle himself speaks of ceaselessly praying for his Gentile converts: for example, Colossians 1:9 states, "We have not ceased praying for you and asking that you may be filled with the knowledge of

God's will in all spiritual wisdom and understanding." I'm pretty sure that other groups along with the Colossians were on his mind. His prayer is constant in the same way that love for one's family is constant.

Third, prayer is one form of several we have for uniting ourselves to our communities and to our past. When we pray together in the congregation, especially when we pray the same prayers every week, we know we are part of a larger group, and there is comfort and strength in that knowledge. When I recite the Hebrew words of the prayer book (in Hebrew, *siddur*), I can hear my mother, father, grandmother reciting those same words, and I can imagine ancestors through the generations saying the words as well. Prayer is a form of generational connection and continuity.

Fourth, communal prayer reminds us that we are not all in the same place—some are joyful while others struggle; some are healthy and others ailing. We may say words that are not, at that very moment, directly relevant to us, but in reciting them, we give support to those who need, at that time, to hear the words. Indeed, various studies suggest that people actually feel better when they know that others are praying for them and with them.

Fifth, prayer is particularly helpful for matters of discernment, whether avoiding temptation on the one hand or making major decisions on the other. Prayer is a form of grounding in helping us think about what God would want for us just as we express what we want from God. The various lines in the Our Father go both ways: they show us God's will even as they help us follow that same will.

Which Version?

The Our Father is not the total of the prayers Jesus's followers prayed, then or subsequently. Nor are the exact words as important as the intent they express. Luke has an alternative version

(Luke 11:2-4), and a third appears in the early Christian text called the *Didache*, or the *Teaching of the Twelve Apostles*. Since we are looking in these six sections at the Sermon on the Mount, we'll look at Matthew's version; on occasion we'll see the Lucan differences.

The fact that there are different versions of the prayer shows us that Jesus's followers remembered it in different ways. The basic meaning is the same in each, but the words differ. And that's good news, since in churches today—depending on the church—the prayer will sound different (consequently, visitors of one Christian tradition can get very confused when they attend worship in the church of a different Christian tradition). Not only do Matthew and Luke offer different versions, even in the English-speaking world there are different translations, and each has a specific nuance. Perhaps most familiar, Roman Catholic communions have "Forgive us our trespasses"; a number of Protestant churches have "Forgive us our debts."

We should not be concerned in this case about who got it right (which implies that someone got it wrong). No one "got it wrong." Jesus may have offered different versions of the prayer; memory is faulty; translation from Jesus's original Aramaic into the Greek of the New Testament introduced additional nuances, as all translation does; the evangelists themselves likely adapted the prayer to fit the needs of their congregations; early scribes had their own concerns, including harmonizing the two versions, and so on. More, as the English language changed, some Christians updated the translations; others retained the familiar King James Version.

We shall never know what the original was or even if there was an original. We can, however, using historical imagination based on solid linguistic information and knowledge of the time, attempt to reconstruct what this prayer, in its Matthean version, might have sounded like to Jesus's disciples. What we find is a magnificent Jewish prayer, echoed in a number of other Jewish prayers *still used to this day*, which offers specific connections to the Jewish tradition and, at the same time, speaks to a universal audience.

"Our Father"

We've already noted that Jewish prayers are often identified by their first words; hence, this prayer is sometimes called the Our Father. In Mrs. Cross's first-grade class, we called it the Lord's Prayer; since I thought the "Lord" in question was the God I knew in the Jewish tradition, I had no problem with the title. I do recall, however, being surprised, after I started asking questions about the Christian tradition, that the "Lord" in the title was Jesus of Nazareth. Who knew?

In Hebrew, "our father" is one word: *avinu*. The *av* part is the same word as the more familiar *abba*, the term Jesus uses to address God in his prayer in Gethsemane: "*Abba*, Father, for you all things are possible; remove this cup from me; yet, not what I want, but what you want" (Mark 14:36). For Jesus, himself at prayer, the address to God as "father" indicates the closeness of the relationship and hence also both what Father and Son have at stake: Jesus, obedient to his Father's will, will go to the cross; his Father, for the sake of humanity (as Jesus states in Matthew 20:28, "just as the Son of Man came not to be served but to serve, and to give his life a ransom for many") will hand his Son over to death.

Paul uses the term twice, each time to assure his Gentile converts that they have now become adopted into the family of Abraham and should now see themselves as children of God. In Romans 8:15-16, talking to his Gentile converts, he writes, "For you did not receive a spirit of slavery to fall back into fear, but you have received a spirit of adoption. When we cry, 'Abba! Father!' it is that very Spirit bearing witness with our spirit that we are children of God." Similarly in Galatians, Paul assures his Gentile readers that "in Christ Jesus you are all children of God through faith"

(3:26) and concludes, "And because you are children, God has sent the Spirit of his Son into our hearts, crying, 'Abba! Father!'" (4:6). As early as Paul, therefore, the Gentile followers of Jesus were calling the God of Israel "Father" and regarding themselves as adopted into the family of Abraham.

In antiquity, to be adopted into a family was a sign of special welcome. Julius Caesar had a biological child with Cleopatra of Egypt, but his heir was his adopted son, Octavian (later, Augustus). We might also think of Jesus as having such a model in his own family since, according to the Gospels of Matthew and Luke, Joseph is not Jesus's biological father, but he cared for Jesus as he would his own biological child.

For Jews, who already recognized their kinship relation, God has always been understood as father as well as king, savior, husband to Israel, and a variety of other titles. For example, the prophet Malachi writes, "Have we not all one father [Hebrew: *av echad*]? Has not one God created us? Why then are we faithless to one another, profaning the covenant of our ancestors?" (2:10). We see here that claiming God as our Father has ethical implications. We are all related; we are family; we are to be faithful to one another as God the Father is faithful to us.

The address to God as "Father" continues to appear in a number of Jewish prayers. One prayer begins "Our father our king"; another is "Father of mercies" or "Merciful father." The prayer for the modern state of Israel begins "Our father, the one in the heavens," which should sound particularly familiar in light of the prayer Jesus teaches in the Sermon on the Mount.

Because of a lack of good historical knowledge, two pieces of misinformation have crept into how we understand these first words. The first is that *abba* at the time of Jesus meant something like "daddy" or "papa," and the second is that Jews would have found such an address for God blasphemous. Whereas in modern Hebrew *abba* can mean "daddy," it did not have that meaning in the Aramaic of Jesus's time. That's why the Greek of the New

Testament correctly translates it as "father." Hardly blasphemous, *abba* was a term other Jews used to address God.

We find a lovely example of this address in the Babylonian Talmud. The story, told in Aramaic, goes as follows:

> Hanan HaNehba was the son of Honi HaMe'aggel's daughter. [This Honi, also known as the Circle-Drawer, was, like Jesus, a miracle-worker who had some control over the weather.] When the world was in need of rain, the Sages [rabbis] would send schoolchildren to him, and they would grab him by the hem of his cloak and say to him: Father, Father [*abba*], give us rain. He said before the Holy One, Blessed be He: Master of the Universe, act on behalf of these children, who cannot distinguish between their Father [*abba*] in Heaven, Who can provide rain, and the father [*abba*] who cannot provide rain. (Taanit 23b)

To call God "Father" is to evoke all the positive images of paternity: God as provider, protector, ever loving and ever compassionate. At the same time, to pray "our father" necessarily connects all those praying as part of the same family.

Finally, for Jesus and his followers, God is the only "father." As Jesus states, "Call no one your father on earth, for you have one Father—the one in heaven" (Matthew 23:9). This comment, and several others, are meant to reconfigure the earthly family. If we all pray to God as father, then we are all siblings, children of the same parent. Jesus goes even "farther" (as it were) by redefining his own family: "For whoever does the will of my Father in heaven is my brother and sister and mother" (Matthew 12:50). For these initial disciples, the group gathered to Jesus and in his name gave their primary loyalty to this new family rather than to their natal family. Demonstrating this new relationship are James and John, who leave their father, Zebedee, in the boat, and join Jesus to go "fish for people" (Matthew 4:19-22).

"[Who is/art] in heaven"

In Mrs. Cross's class, I was initially confused. Our prayer began, "Our Father, who art in heaven." My initial thought was that God's name was Art, like Art Fleming, the original host of *Jeopardy*. But then there was this Harold fellow (we'll get to him). The NRSV, however, has simply "Our father in heaven." Art disappeared.

The "art" comes from the King James Version. While many people today are happy with updated Bibles and so updated liturgies, when it comes to the Our Father, suddenly people in the 2020s sound like they just stepped out of the seventeenth century. And yet, we've adapted that too, since the King James Version offers not "who art in heaven" but "which art in heaven." At least we've adapted our relative pronouns. The Greek, translated literally and therefore somewhat awkwardly, is "who [is] in the heavens," with "heavens" being plural. As we've seen before, all translators are traitors.

I understand why many people like the "who art" language: it gives the impression of formality; if we are to talk to God, some think, then we should be on our best behavior. If we dress up for church (something increasingly going out of fashion, literally), then we should speak in a more formal manner as well. Yet for the initial readers of the King James Version, the language was no more and no less formal than any average conversation. When Juliet asks her new boyfriend, "Wherefore art thou Romeo," she was casual, not formal (nor, by the way, was she asking him where he was from). Thus, the language was not originally meant to be formal.

Moreover, if we are to address God as "father," then we don't need the formality. We should be able to speak with God, and to God, as we would to our parents (presuming a very healthy family relationship; here I think not only of my good relationship with my parents but of how I would want my children to relate to me).

On the "heavens," part of the first line, we find both Mediterranean cosmology and modern civics. The ancient Jewish cosmos had more than one heaven; that's why Paul can write, "I know a person in Christ who fourteen years ago was caught up to the third heaven—whether in the body or out of the body I do not know; God knows" (2 Corinthians 12:2). Since there are in some ancient cosmologies seven heavens and in others ten, Paul is here being modest.

In terms of civics, to identify God as the "Father in the heavens" is to make a political statement. The Roman Senate awarded Julius Caesar the title *pater patriae*, Latin for "father of the fatherland"; his heir, Augustus, received the same title. Ovid, the poet famous for his *Metamorphoses*, hailed Augustus: "Thou bear on earth the name which Jupiter bears in high heaven: of men thou art the father, he of the gods."[1] Granted, being named by the Senate "Father of the Fatherland" eventually became a cheapened title; among its holders were Caligula and Nero, not among the empire's best efforts. Tiberius, the ruler at the time of Jesus's adult life (so Luke 3:1, "in the fifteenth year of the reign of Emperor Tiberius"), was reputed to have rejected the title, but by the 30s of the Common Era, it was known across the empire.

Thus, when the followers of Jesus talked about their Father in the heavens, they were making a political statement. The "father of the fatherland" was not the ultimate authority; the Father in the heavens was. Jesus will later tell his disciples, "You know that the rulers of the Gentiles lord it over them, and their great ones are tyrants over them" because that's the way the world works. In God's kingdom, Jesus continues, "It will not be so among you; but whoever wishes to be great among you must be your servant" (Matthew 20:25-26).

I had a great relationship with my dad; he died of a heart attack when I was still quite young, but I treasure the memories I have of him. Yet I am also aware of people whose fathers were distant or absent or abusive, and for them to pray "our father" conjures all the wrong images. Still others, with the same experiences, find comfort in the idea of the Father in heaven as the trustworthy model.

Awareness of how "father" language impacts us all differently can help in mutual understanding, as can alternative wording. One New Zealand version begins, "Eternal Spirit, / Earth-maker, Pain-bearer, Life-giver."[2]

Several new versions begin with some variant of "Our Father, Our Mother . . ." I suspect Jesus would be happy if the wording acknowledged God as caring and compassionate, as in relationship with the entire community, and as above any earthly authority. The words "Our Father who is in the heavens" does all that and more.

"Hallowed be your name"

Given that I've already fussed about "who art" rather than "who is," don't be surprised that that I'm not thrilled with "thy" name. It was a normal way of speaking in Shakespearean English, but unless we want to sound like Shakespeare all the time, we might as well update. Granted, a number of students have pushed back on this point: they claim that the King James Version is the "authorized version" (as it says on every title page) and therefore should be the one used. However, the text is not authorized by God; it was authorized by the King of England. Further, if one insists that the only way of saying the prayer is by using the King James Version, then everyone in the world would need to use this translation. So much for the Germans, the French, the Masai, and the Aleut.

As for the more substantive parts of the verse, "Harold be your name" made sense to me; "Hallowed" not so much (who is named "Hallowed"?)—hence the problem with having a twentieth-century child read a seventeenth-century translation of a first-century prayer. Happily, history resolved this concern and several others.

Hallowing—making sacred or sanctifying the divine name—is a component of most Jewish prayers. The Hebrew term for "sacred" is based on the root k-d-sh. The prayer said before drinking a glass of wine is called the Kiddush; the prayer most familiar as the one recited by those in mourning is the Aramaic Kaddish. The term *hallowed* also comes into other expressions, most famously "Halloween"—"holy eve"—the "sacred evening" dedicated to the saints.

Sanctifying the divine name appears as early as the Psalms. For example, Psalm 105:1-3 exclaims,

> O give thanks to the LORD, call on his name,
>> make known his deeds among the peoples.
> Sing to him, sing praises to him;
>> tell of all his wonderful works.
> Glory in his holy name;
>> let the hearts of those who seek the LORD rejoice.

Rabbinic commentary on this Psalm enhances this hallowing or sanctification. The Midrash on Psalm 25:13 similarly begins, "May his great name grow exalted and glorified" (my translation).

The concept of hallowing the divine name in Jewish liturgy is particularly prominent in the Kaddish, an Aramaic (yes, the language Jesus spoke) prayer that begins, "Magnified [*yitgadal*] and sanctified [or hallowed; *v'yitkadash*—you can see the *k-d-sh* root] be [God's] great name [*shmei raba*]."

For Jesus's invocation, "Hallowed be your name," we still have to ask *who* is doing the hallowing. The verse could be an invocation that God step into history again, as happened at the Exodus, to ensure that God's name, rather than that of Caesar (or any other political leader, athlete, movie star . . .), receives praise and attention. In this construct, God does the hallowing. Or perhaps it is a prayer for the world to come, the kingdom of heaven, the time when all people praise God.

The two options are compatible. In fact, I think hallowing the divine name means allowing God to be God rather than constraining God into any theological box. The name of God, according to Exodus 3:14, is *eheyeh asher eheyeh*, "I will be what I will be" (the NRSV rather flatly translates, "I AM WHO I AM" (although at least they provide all capital letters, a form ancient Hebrew lacks). The

English translation suggests determination of identity. (I cannot help being reminded of Popeye the Sailor Man, who insisted, "I yam what I yam" in confirming his identity.)

The Hebrew testifies to divine freedom. God will be whatever God will be: a father or mother (since the Bible also offers maternal images), older brother, wise aunt, master, rock, spring, suffering servant, redeemer. This freedom also means that God can be part of a conversation: Abraham debated with God regarding whether to destroy Sodom and Gomorrah; God heard Job's cry for justice and responded. Similarly the Canaanite woman in Matthew 15:21-28 convinces Jesus to heal her demon-possessed daughter (this passage, in which Jesus appears resistant to healing, is another topic deserving its lesson). The point of this list, to which other biblical accounts can be added, is that God is free; no theological determination or personal theology can box God in.

When the Hebrew Scriptures were translated into Greek, that imperfect irregular Hebrew verb *eheyeh* becomes *ego eimi*, "I am." Consequently, when Jesus says, in John's Gospel, "I am the bread of life" or "I am the true vine," Greek speakers would hear an echo of Exodus 3. The shift is a linguistic one: Greek thought preferred the permanent, the unchanging; Hebrew thought preferred the open possibility. Readers today have a choice: What kind of God should we proclaim?

"Your kingdom come"

Jews then and still today speak of "the world to come," a time marked by universal peace. As the Aleinu, another ancient prayer still recited today, hopes, "On that day his name shall be one." Rather than focus on time, Jesus focuses on place: he uses "kingdom" rather than "world."

We should take "kingdom" language seriously because he, not we, lived in a kingdom, without democracy, ruled by an emperor and maintained by an army. "Your kingdom come" has a palpable political edge, as does "our Father, the one who is in the heavens." Such political concerns are not antithetical to theology, and America's famous "separation of church and state" does not mean that churches should be silent in the face of oppression. Jesus takes his place among the prophets of Israel, prophets such as Isaiah and Jeremiah and Amos, who challenged the kings of their time. By praying in the imperative, as if one is ordering God—"[Make] your kingdom come!"—one clearly states that the Roman Empire, with Herod Antipas (the client king in Galilee) and Pontius Pilate (the governor in Judea), is not what God's kingdom looks like.

To the contrary, Matthew has given us examples of people who are already entering the kingdom of heaven by acting on behalf of others: Joseph who marries the pregnant Mary and then protects her and her child by relocating from Bethlehem to Egypt and then to Nazareth; the people who come to Jesus for healing and, more, their caregivers; the disciples who come to Jesus for instruction; the woman who anoints Jesus; the centurion at the cross; the women who come to the tomb; and many more.

"Be done your will, as in heaven even on earth" (my translation)

Jesus models how to discern God's will, but in his case, the modeling is something his fellow Jews already knew. To discern God's will, begin with God's Word, the Scriptures of Israel.

In the temptation narrative (Matthew 4:1-11), Satan attempts to get Jesus to use his powers for personal gain rather than public good. At times, he even cites biblical texts to support his efforts. (It was Shakespeare who said that the devil can quote scripture to his own purposes, but Matthew anticipated that quotation by a millennium and a half.) Jesus responds to each of the three temptations by citing Deuteronomy, the New Testament's most quoted book of the Pentateuch. In other words (literally), Jesus tells us that the place to discern the divine will is in the Torah: begin with the text and then determine what it means to you, and to your community, in your own context.

The Sermon on the Mount has already made this point, several times. Toward the beginning, Jesus insists that he has not come to do away with the Torah and the Prophets; then, he cites the texts and extends their meaning: from do not murder to do not be angry; from do not commit adultery to do not lust, and so on. To determine divine will, such that we can enact it ourselves—if we do, God's will *in heaven* becomes manifest *even on earth*—we study the Word of God and then engage with others on how to understand it.

More, Jesus follows Abraham, Moses, Job, and many others in demonstrating how, sometimes, divine will is not what we will. On the night he will be arrested, "he threw himself on the ground and prayed, 'My Father, if it is possible, let this cup pass from me; yet not what I want but what you want'" (Matthew 26:39). Hearing this verse, readers recall chapter 6, where "our Father" is also Jesus's Father: we see Jesus in prayer, and he prays that God's will be done. Finally, the prayer allows, indeed encourages, the disciples to speak aloud what is in their hearts. And giving voice to one's desires makes those desires both real and shared.

"Give us this day our daily bread"

In its English translation, the verse is redundant: "this day" and "daily" mean the same thing. "Give us our daily bread" would be fine; so would "Give us this day our bread." I recall the tautology "hot water heater": if the water is already hot, why does it need to be heated? So too, if the bread comes daily why the need to say "this day"? The problem in English is the seeming repetition, and the problem is rooted in the Greek word *epiousios*, translated "daily."

The term is new to the New Testament, so translators need to figure out what it means. *Epi* is a suffix; *ousia* is the verb. If we imagine or, technically, retro-translate the two terms back into

Jesus's Aramaic, we get something that suggests "for tomorrow" or "for the future." Now the verse makes sense. Jesus invites his disciples to ask, "Give us tomorrow's bread today," a request that gives us a hint of the original takeaway (to continue the food metaphor).

Some ancient Jewish texts portray heaven as a glorious banquet: in the world to come, we eat, for this is the time when no one goes hungry and when we recline at a banquet with our family and friends through the centuries. Speaking of the time of salvation and referring to Mount Zion, Isaiah writes,

> On this mountain the LORD of hosts will make for all
> peoples,
>> a feast of rich food, a feast of well-aged wines,
>> of rich food filled with marrow, of well-aged wines
>> strained clear.
>
> . . . .
> It will be said on that day,
>> Lo, this is our God; we have waited for him, so that he
>> might save us.
>> This is the LORD for whom we have waited;
>> let us be glad and rejoice in his salvation. (25:6, 9)

Jesus himself predicts, "Many will come from east and west and will eat with Abraham and Isaac and Jacob in the kingdom of heaven" (Matthew 8:11).

That "daily bread" has another earlier reference, for it reminds us of the manna in the wilderness, the daily bread God provided the Israelites as they journeyed from slavery to freedom (Exodus 16). This image brings its own connotations: manna was not to be hoarded, and neither is bread, for it will go stale and become inedible. Sharing, rather than hoarding, is the mark of a functional community. And thoughts of manna, in turn, anticipate a later verse in the prayer. In Exodus 16:4, God says to Moses, "I am going to rain bread from heaven for you, and each day the people shall go out and gather enough for that day. In that way I will test them, whether they will follow my instruction or not." There's a connection among God's testing Israel with manna, the prayer for bread each day, the hope that we not be "led into temptation" or "brought to the test," and, to extend to John's Gospel, Jesus as the bread of life. And so we learn that those who break bread together, or those who share the same loaf, are part of a community that extends back into antiquity and forward to that heavenly banquet. And that gives much to chew on.

"Give us this day our daily bread" thus likely meant in its original Aramaic "Give us tomorrow's bread today—bring about your rule, when we can eat at the messianic banquet." This is the prophetic hope, the prophetic vision. And this is why Jesus continually meets people at table, so much so that I suspect he was on the chubby side. He feeds five thousand and then another four thousand, at least, for after each notice, Matthew remarks, "besides women and children" (14:21; 15:38).

Jesus dines with sinners and tax collectors, and so he risks questioning by others who wonder why he is associating with the ancient equivalents of traitors, loan sharks, drug dealers, and pimps. His view: they, too, are members of the community and need to be called to repentance. His is not a table that excludes anyone.

He has a significant meal at both the beginning and end of Holy Week. At the beginning, an unnamed woman anoints him for his burial, and he proclaims that the story will be told "in remembrance of her" (Matthew 26:12-13). At the end—his Last Supper—he institutes the ritual to be done in his name:

> While they were eating, Jesus took a loaf of bread, and after blessing it he broke it, gave it to the disciples, and said, "Take, eat; this is my body." Then he took a cup, and after giving thanks he gave it to them, saying, "Drink from it, all of you; for this is my blood of the covenant, which is poured out for many for the forgiveness of sins." (vv. 26-28)

At the synagogue, after we welcome the Sabbath, we serve food. Why? Because the Sabbath is a foretaste—literally—of the world to come. For the church, the Communion or Eucharist is part of this celebration.

He tells parables about banquets, including insisting that his disciples invite to the table not just their friends or those who can reciprocate but any who need daily bread (for example, Matthew 22:9). Reading through Matthew, or any of the Gospels, should make one not only spiritually hungry for more stories, and more theology, but also for actual food, preferably bread shared with others.

In reading Matthew, we have encountered references to bread already, and those should resonate with the prayer. For example, Satan's first temptation to a starving Jesus who has not eaten for forty days is, "Command these stones to become loaves of bread" (4:3). Jesus responds, "It is written, 'One does not live by *bread alone*, but by every word that comes from the mouth of God'" (4:4, quoting Deuteronomy 8:3, italics added). The entire verse from Deuteronomy reads, "He humbled you by letting you hunger, then by feeding you with manna, with which neither you nor your ancestors were acquainted, in order to make you understand that one does not live by bread alone, but by every word that comes from the mouth of the LORD." Thus, daily bread cannot be separated from the Word of God as encountered in the Scripture. The Gospel of John makes this point visceral when it connects the incarnate *logos*, the Word, with bread: Jesus states, "I am the bread of life. Whoever comes to me will never be hungry, and whoever believes in me will never be thirsty. . . . I am the bread of life. . . . I am the living bread that came down from heaven. Whoever eats of this bread will live forever; and the bread that I will give for the life of the world is my flesh" (6:35, 48, 51).

Along with allusions and parables and rituals, "daily bread" has a very practical reference. It also means, "Dear Father, please give us enough food to get us through the day so that we and our children will not starve." The prayer asks for bread, sustenance, a staple of life for those in the Middle East. The prayer reminds disciples who are in comfortable settings that not everyone gets the daily bread; to love God and to love neighbor mandates that hungry bellies be fed. For those who feast while others starve, there's a lovely parable in Luke's Gospel about a rich man "who feasted sumptuously every day" (16:19) whereas at his gates a poor man yearned for the crumbs. It doesn't go well for the rich man.

"And forgive us our debts, as we also have forgiven our debtors"

In Mrs. Cross's class, we prayed, "Forgive us our trespasses"; this was also the version used in the majority Roman Catholic town. The reference to "trespasses" occurs right after the Our Father in Matthew's Gospel, where Jesus states, "For if you forgive others their trespasses, your heavenly Father will also forgive you; but if you do not forgive others, neither will your Father forgive your trespasses" (6:14-15). But for the prayer itself, Matthew reads not "forgive us our trespasses" but "forgive us our debts."

By glossing the prayer with two lines regarding trespasses, Matthew makes clear that "debts" is a synonym for "trespasses." Confirming this connection among sin, debt, and trespass is the parallel prayer in Luke's Gospel, which reads, "And forgive us our sins, / for we ourselves forgive everyone indebted to us" (11:4). Adventures in translation explain how we get from debt to sin to trespass; they also open questions about the relationship of economic debt to sin and of release of economic debt to forgiveness.

Jesus spoke Aramaic, and the Aramaic word *chob* or *choba* can be translated "sin," "debt," and "trespass." The various definitions relate to the need to explain sin, which is not simply an abstract concept. "Sin" in Hebrew thought has actual content—it is a "thing"—and so metaphors were needed to understand it.

Sin was imaged variously. It could be a burden that in forgiveness is lifted off. We see how this metaphor functions in our own body language: people who realize they have hurt another will sometimes walk as if they are bearing a physical burden and not just a burden of conscience; when they are forgiven, they stand up straight. Sin could be a stain that required being washed off, hence the 1878 hymn by Elisha A. Hoffman, "Are You Washed in the Blood?" In turn, the hymn is based on Revelation 7:14, where one of the heavenly elders points out "they who have come out of the great ordeal; they have washed their robes and made them white in the blood of the Lamb." Sacrificial blood was like detergent, and it could remove the stain of sin.

Sin was also imagined as a debt, as if we all had heavenly bank accounts, and when we sinned, the account became drained. Forgiveness restores the balance, literally, between humanity and divinity as well as among members of a community. This metaphor also underlies other comments in the Sermon on the Mount, such as this verse following the prayer: "Do not store up for yourselves treasures on earth, where moth and rust consume and where thieves break in and steal; but store up for yourselves treasures in heaven, where neither moth nor rust consumes and where thieves do not break in and steal. For where your treasure is, there your heart will be also" (Matthew 6:19-21; we'll return to this metaphor in the next chapter).

The metaphor of sin as debt works in Aramaic and Hebrew; it was not, however, common in Greek (some idioms translate; others do not). Because Matthew understood the prayer in terms of debt, it is likely that, somewhere in the tradition, Jesus's followers remembered that he was concerned not only about forgiving sins that people commit against each other and against God but also about economic justice.

Hints of this concern appear elsewhere in the Gospels. For example, earlier in the Sermon on the Mount, Jesus advised, "Give to everyone who begs from you, and do not refuse anyone who wants to borrow from you" (Matthew 5:42); in his synagogue sermon in Luke 4:18-19, Jesus invokes the idea of the Jubilee Year (see Isaiah 61:1), the time when all debts are forgiven:

"The Spirit of the Lord is upon me,
　　because he has anointed me
　　　　to bring good news to the poor.

. . . .

to proclaim the year of the Lord's favor."

Matthew's parable of the laborers in the vineyard (20:1-15) depicts a landowner who provides all the workers, regardless of what time they entered the vineyard, what we would call a "living wage."[3]

"Your will be done on earth as it is in heaven" means that if someone needs, another will provide. When that will is done, then no longer will the prophets need to lament, "'Alas for you who heap up what is not your own!' / How long will you load yourselves with goods taken in pledge?" (Habakkuk 2:6). When we act as God would act, we give freely and generously because that is what God does. It would be hypocritical to say to God, "Your will be done," and then not do it ourselves. And when we do not act generously, the parable of the unforgiving servant (Matthew 18:23-35) makes clear the negative consequences.

To forgive sins helps the community relate; to forgive debts does the same since, in both cases, no one person is in a position to lord it over another. But neither should the community in Jesus's name allow themselves to be victims of those who seek to cheat or to take advantage. Matthew also includes forms of discipline for those who would abuse community generosity (see especially Matthew 18). Jesus is not calling people to be doormats. To turn the cheek for a slap, to strip to give away the cloak in the court room, and to go the extra mile is to confront injustice, not to tolerate it. The same holds for forgiving debt and forgiving sin.

"And do not bring us to the time of trial"

There are at least three versions of this verse: "Do not bring us to the time of trial," "Lead us not into temptation," and from Mrs. Cross's class, "Lead us not into Penn Station." Putting the third option aside, we can easily explain the first two. In Greek, the verb *peiradzō* and the noun *peirasmos* can be translated as both "temptation" and "test" or "trial." Both translations make sense because a test can become a temptation, especially if we think about cheating in order to pass, if we seek for shortcuts for our own advantage rather than for the benefit of others, or if we take the easy road rather than the narrow path that leads to salvation. (I'm anticipating here the ending of the Sermon on the Mount in Matthew 7:13-14.)

Matthew, brilliant writer that he is, has prepared us for this verse in the Sermon by describing an earlier test or temptation. That to which we do not want to be led is a cognate of the term describing Jesus's being "tempted" or "tested" by Satan, an event that, according to Matthew's Gospel, comes only two chapters before the prayer. Matthew 4:1 states, "Then Jesus was led up by the Spirit into the wilderness to be tempted by the devil." Reinforcing the tempting/test, Matthew then identifies Satan "the tempter" who says to Jesus, "If you are the Son of God, command these stones to become loaves of bread" (4:3). Jesus passes the test and does not succumb to this temptation, despite his hunger, by quoting Deuteronomy 8:3: "One does not live by bread alone, but by every word that comes from the mouth of the LORD." Immediately we (should) recall the previous verse about "daily bread" or "tomorrow's bread." Good Jewish teacher that he is, Jesus doesn't ask of his disciples anything he does not already ask of himself.

Later in the Gospel, Pharisees (in the narrative role of Satan—another problem for another series, perhaps) also test Jesus. In Matthew 16:1, Pharisees together with Sadducees ask him for a sign from heaven, and Jesus responds enigmatically with another biblical reference, this time to the "sign of Jonah." In 19:3, "some Pharisees came to him, and to test him they asked, 'Is it lawful for a man to divorce his wife for any cause?'" The question echoes one of the extensions we encountered in the Sermon on the Mount, and Jesus's answer again appeals to Scripture.

In 22:17, Pharisees, now paired with Herodians, ask Jesus

about the legality of paying Roman taxes. Jesus himself names the intent of the question: "Why are you putting me to the test, you hypocrites?" (v. 18). His answer, which begins with the discussion of the image on the coin and concludes with the famous "Render unto Caesar" (KJV), implies additional scriptural references, including the forbidding of idolatry and the making of graven images. Finally, in verse 36, a lawyer, seeking to "test him," asks Jesus, "Which commandment in the law is the greatest?" Jesus responds by citing Deuteronomy 6 on love of God and Leviticus 19 on love of neighbor.

Having passed all these tests, Jesus then comes to his greatest test: the threat of the cross, a death he does not wish either for himself or for his followers. Hence, in Gethsemane, he again instructs them about prayer: "Stay awake and pray that you may not come into the time of trial [same word as in the Our Father prayer]; the spirit indeed is willing, but the flesh is weak" (Matthew 26:41, and yes, that last line is in fact the Bible, not Shakespeare).

A number of my students are disturbed by the idea that God would somehow test us; testing, it seems to them, is the role of Satan (or perhaps their professor, but I'd prefer not to go down that road). My students are not the only ones to be disturbed by this idea. The verse was so sufficiently confusing, and controversial, that the Epistle of James, a letter that has numerous allusions to the Sermon on the Mount, already addresses it: "No one, when tempted, should say, 'I am being tempted by God'; for God cannot be tempted by evil and he himself tempts no one. But one is tempted by one's own desire, being lured and enticed by it" (1:13-14).

Following this idea, in 2019 Pope Francis approved a new translation of the *Roman Missal* prepared by the Italian Bishops' Conference. The translation replaces the famous "lead us not into temptation" with "do not let us fall into temptation" or "do not abandon us to temptation."

I understand the rationale for this shift, and it is consistent with James 1:13-14. And yet . . . Scripture does tell us that God tests us. For example, in Genesis 22:1, God tests Abraham by commanding him to sacrifice his son. God also allowed "the Satan" to test Job, and Job was not happy about the results.

At the same time, God gives us the resources to overcome temptation. That is Matthew's point (or at least one of them) in depicting Jesus quoting the Torah—the primary resource for avoiding evil—in his defeat of Satan. The Babylonian Talmud offers a similar prayer: "And may it be Your will, O Lord my God, to accustom me in Your Torah, attach me to Your mitzvot, and lead me not into transgression, nor into error, nor into iniquity, nor into temptation nor into disgrace" (Berakhot 60b).

"Do not bring us to the test" can thus be summarized: let us not be tempted to use our resources just for ourselves; let us not come to a place where we lord it over others rather than engage in servant leadership; let us not desire the splendors of the world rather than attend to its needs. If such temptations come, and they will, we know we have the resources to resist and to overcome: the Scriptures, the community, the Spirit, and our own conscience.

"but rescue us from the evil one"

In Mrs. Cross's class, the prayer ended, "And deliver us from evil." The NRSV is likely closer to the Greek: *ho poneros*, literally, "the evil one." Jesus lived in a time and place in which the "evil one"—Satan, the devil—was part of the worldview. Satan has already tempted Jesus, and Jesus shows that rescue is possible. We do not have to succumb to temptation, and calling upon divine help reminds us that the help is always there.

Once again, in a brilliant narrative move, Matthew will reference Satan. After Jesus tells his disciples that he "must go to Jerusalem and undergo great suffering . . . and be killed" (16:21), Peter responds, "God forbid it!" (v. 22). But this is Jesus's fate, a fate he accepts despite his great desire not to die. Jesus responds, "Get behind me, Satan! You are a stumbling block to me; for you are setting your mind not on divine things but on human things" (v. 23). Peter is tempting Jesus to leave the path set out for him. And Jesus, once again, overcomes temptation.

"Deliver us from evil" makes more sense to many today for whom "Satan" is just a metaphor rather than an actual being. Here we need to avoid the temptation of condemning people who hold one view as opposed to the other: people who believe in Satan should not be dismissed as silly or superstitious; people who do not should not be condemned as antibiblical or atheistic.

As time went on, views of Satan in Jewish and Christian contexts diverged. The Jewish tradition came to see Satan primarily in his role in Job: a being in the heavenly court who tests people, usually righteous people; he is also usually defeated, and his defeat demonstrates the righteousness of the person tested. Christianity—in part because of the temptation narratives in the Synoptic Gospels, the notice in Luke 22:3 and John 13:27 that Satan motivated Judas Iscariot to betray Jesus, and the satanic figures in the Book of Revelation—generally came to regard Satan as an evil being to be defeated by Jesus, finally, at the Parousia, his Second Coming.

Some of us may not believe in Satan in the sense of an actual, supernatural, malevolent being who possesses people so that they act in destructive ways. "The Devil made me do it" can function as a denial of personal responsibility. Personally, I don't need a Satan to recognize those things in the world that tempt us: drugs, alcohol, gambling, pornography, and so on. But we do need resources to overcome addictions, and the prayer is precisely such a resource.

"For thine is the kingdom, and the power, and the glory, for ever. Amen"

This final verse appears neither in Matthew nor Luke; it comes from the *Didache*, which I mentioned earlier, the Syriac translation of the Bible (the Peshitta), and a number of other early manuscripts. The *Didache* also ends the prayer with the exhortation "Thrice in the day thus pray." Prayers do not record such "words of praise" (Greek: *doxology*), although this liturgical conclusion does have aesthetic appeal.

Ascribing to God "kingdom," "power," and "glory" returns the prayer to its opening concerns, from the title "Father" to the concern for that other "kingdom" to come. If we recognize that these political terms refer to something theological rather than human, we are better able to challenge injustice in the present. If we do that well, then we do not have to pray for bread since everyone will have enough to eat; we will not have to pray for divine will to be done on earth since everyone will love their neighbors, and as Jesus would have it, their enemies as well. To that, "amen" is the best response.

Chapter 5

FINDING YOUR TREASURE

After the Prayer

Rather than jump right into whatever problem requires fixing, whatever puzzle needs solving, or whatever hurt requires comforting, many people take a moment to center themselves. Prayer, meditation, a few deep breaths—all these exercises and more help us do what needs to be done in a more caring, more thoughtful manner. Hence, Matthew presents the prayer as a centering for the disciples: Start here, the Gospel suggests, and anything that follows will be easier to complete or to bear.

The approach is solid. It begins with recognizing that none of us is alone, for we can all pray to "our Father." Knowing that this Father is in heaven gives a sense of abiding presence since heaven is not restricted to a particular setting on earth. Hallowing the divine name reminds us that there is something greater than us, and so we have at least two helpful conclusions: (1) we are not divine and, therefore, do not have the power to solve all problems, and (2) the prayer points to God, reminding us that the focus is not on us or for us. The prayer combats egocentrism, even as it encourages everyone who recites its words.

"Your kingdom come, your will be done, on earth as it is in heaven" teaches us that there is a reason we fix those problems and comfort those hurts, even when we might rather be doing something else. Personally, I'd rather be playing with my puppy, finishing the sweater I have been knitting for my son, or sharing a glass of wine with my husband than grading the eighty-plus final exams from the New Testament Intro course. But once we realize we are doing something that fits what we know is heaven's will, we can at least get done what needs to get done.

"Daily bread" becomes palpable when we share a meal and take the time to consider how many people were involved in getting the food to our tables. When we eat, we are part of a larger community. All this, plus hope for that heavenly banquet, is already nourishment for the body and the spirit.

Forgiving debts, or sins, is difficult. Economically, people sometimes need the money they lent to others. Emotionally, for some people, crimes and insults are unforgivable, and they should *not* be told they are a bad Christian if their hearts are not in a position to forgive. But a simple takeaway that most people can appreciate is that the verse prepares us to be in a right relationship with the world: "as we also have forgiven our debtors" means we forego the tendency to say, "You owe me."

Avoiding temptation and being delivered from evil or, if you prefer, the evil one is the best ending. We are tempted to procrastinate, to rush through the work rather than proceed with care, to ignore what should be addressed if we want that divine will to be done on earth. So anyone, Christian, Jew—anyone—could recite this prayer, find a center, recognize priorities, and then be prepared to find the treasure that awaits.

Fasting

It might sound initially odd to think of fasting as the first step in finding one's treasure. On second thought, it should make good sense. When we give to charity, we are reminded that there are people in need and that we might at some point, given economic changes, catastrophic medical bills, or emergency, require help from others. In the same way, when one fasts—here I mean people who have sufficient resources and are otherwise healthy and not suffering from an eating disorder—one immediately recognizes that there are people in need of food; we feel that need viscerally.

Fasting has other healthy aspects, all of which help us find our treasure. For example, fasting helps us, in terms of personal discipline, learn that we can control our stomachs rather than have our stomachs control us. Fasting, especially communal fasting, has a long biblical history in relation to repentance. Judaism has a number of fast days during the calendar year, of which the most important and best known is Yom Kippur, the Day of Atonement, when from sundown to sundown the community comes together to fast, to pray, and to atone. The prayers, in community, actually help us through the fast, as we think about our relationships with others and with God. Similarly, my Muslim friends who fast from sunrise to sunset in the month of Ramadan find an experience of community solidarity and renewal as well as of self-discipline.

Increasingly, I have been encountering Protestant Christians who practice fasting, or modified forms of fasting, in solidarity with those who do not have enough to eat. Instead of lunch, or a dessert, they dedicate the cost of the food to a food bank.

Finally, fasting has become a nonviolent way of engaging in protest when freedom is lacking. The technical term here is "hunger strike." In pre-Christian Ireland, fasting people would station themselves at the door of the person who had committed some injustice against them; the fasting indicated the reverse of hospitality and was intended to shame the perpetrator into recompense, or reconciliation. A similar practice can be found in India, dating as far back as the *Ramayana*, an ancient Hindu text. More recent examples include British and American suffragettes, Mohandas Gandhi, Irish nationalists, and Cubans imprisoned because of opposition to Fidel Castro. In several of these cases, people died either from medical complications of being force-fed or from the fasting itself.

Thus, the fast as protest can be seen as a form of taking up one's cross (see Matthew 10:38; 16:24).

We've already noted that Jesus does not ask of his followers anything he would not do himself. Before his temptation by Satan in the wilderness, Jesus fasted for forty days and nights (4:2). Yet Jesus also recognizes that there is a time to fast as well as a time to feast. Indeed, he and his disciples were not known for the practice of fasting. Instead, Matthew records that John the Baptist's disciples asked Jesus, "Why do we and the Pharisees fast often, but your disciples do not fast?" (9:14). Jesus's response takes a metaphorical approach: "The wedding guests cannot mourn as long as the bridegroom is with them, can they? The days will come when the bridegroom is taken away from them, and then they will fast" (9:15). Jesus himself fasted, and he anticipated that his disciples would also fast; at the same time, he wanted his disciples, in his presence, to sense the joy they would have at a wedding, with food and wine and the uniting of families.

The question then becomes: how do you fast? Jesus has already warned his disciples about practicing their piety for show (6:1). Now he gives another example on how to avoid such hypocrisy:

> "Whenever you fast, do not look dismal, like the hypocrites,
> for they disfigure their faces so as to show others that they
> are fasting. Truly I tell you, they have received their reward.
> But when you fast, put oil on your head and wash your face,
> so that your fasting may be seen not by others but by your
> Father who is in secret; and your Father who sees in secret
> will reward you." (vv. 16-18)

Fasting is designed to master the body and so overcome the ego; to make fasting "all about me" is to defeat the purpose. One is not to "feed on" the admiration or pity of others.

A final comment, this one of concern. I've met a number of individuals over the past forty years who have taken Jesus's forty-day fast, his prediction that his followers will fast, and the idea of fasting in secret as Jesus's permission, indeed his encouragement, to engage in extreme fasting. These individuals, mostly young women, then hide their fasting from their families. They pretend to eat, or they will eat and then regurgitate whatever they consume. Pastors and Bible study leaders would do well to use these verses as prompts to speak about anorexia and bulimia, to show the difference between healthy and unhealthy fasting, and to point out to friends and families the warning signs of eating disorders.

Storing Up Treasures

If we have the ability to control our bodies, then we also have the ability to control our stuff. That control underlies the contrast between earthly wealth and heavenly treasures. We need food, but we need more, as Jesus told Satan, "One does not live by bread alone" (4:4). Similarly, we need stuff—shelter, some form of transportation for long distances, clothing, and so on (making a list of what we think we "need" is often salutary; it's great for downsizing). But stuff—possessions, wealth, mammon—is insufficient, just as bread is insufficient.

Stuff cannot save us. Instead, it draws us in. Human beings are acquisitive individuals, and we generally find it easier to take in than to give away. Those of us who have known poverty and hunger want more stuff because we know what it is like to be without, and we never want to experience that feeling again. The problem then becomes that we can never have enough. Those of us who have children work and save because we want to give those children everything we did not have or everything we think will make their lives easier. Another problem arises: we can never leave them enough. Some people have concluded that money can buy happiness, and they do their best to prove the point only to find that they must take yet another vacation or have yet another car, home, painting, coin, or whatever they collect.

The author of Ecclesiastes got it right: "The lover of money will not be satisfied with money; nor the lover of wealth, with gain. This also is vanity" (5:10). First Timothy 6:10 puts the problem in stark terms: "The love of money is a root of all kinds of evil, and in their eagerness to be rich some have wandered away from the faith and pierced themselves with many pains." Jesus, understanding how we can become enslaved to the body and enslaved to stuff, insists: "No one can serve two masters; for a slave will either hate the one and love the other, or be devoted to the one and despise the other. You cannot serve God and [mammon]" (Matthew 6:24; see also Luke 16:13, where this line follows the parable of the dishonest steward). Matthew retained the Aramaic term and, by doing so, may have hinted to readers that mammon, that foreign-sounding power, was some sort of deity. In each case, the NRSV (less than helpfully) reads, "you cannot serve God and wealth."

By translating the word *mammon*, the NRSV strips from these verses a great deal of their import. To Greek speakers (and perhaps to English speakers today), setting God in opposition to mammon—an unfamiliar term—makes mammon, or all of our *stuff*, sound more like another god or idol. More, the Aramaic term *mammon* comes from the root *'-m-n*, which means "trust" or "reliance." Hence the irony: one cannot rely on, cannot trust, stuff.

In the Sermon on the Mount, Jesus refocuses the question of stuff from earth to the heavens. He has already instructed his disciples to pray, "Your will be done, on earth as it is in heaven" (Matthew 6:10). Now he provides another link between heaven (the ideal) and earth (the actual) to show how the two can be harmonized. He instructs, "Do not store up for yourselves treasures on earth, where moth and rust consume and where thieves break in and steal; but store up for yourselves treasures in heaven, where neither moth nor rust consumes and where thieves do not break in and steal. For where your treasure is, there your heart will be also" (vv. 19-21).

"Treasure on earth" is, in this context, just what it sounds like. Jesus is not talking about a good reputation gained from a life of generosity and compassion, which is something to be treasured. He is talking about stuff, stuff that can be destroyed by human and natural forces. Stuff can be stolen; banks can fail. Stuff can be ruined by moths and termites, rust and rot. Stuff cannot ultimately protect us, and we cannot ultimately protect it. There's even a parable about lost stuff: "The kingdom of heaven is like treasure hidden in a field, which someone found and hid; then in his joy he goes and sells all that he has and buys that field" (13:44). The person who did the hiding attempted to "store up . . . treasures on earth," and that didn't work. However, the one who found the treasure will now have to figure out what to do with it.

The idea of storing up treasures on earth brings us back, again, to the Our Father prayer. To pray "as we also have forgiven our debtors" (6:12) means to forego collecting what is due.

We could list the numerous passages elsewhere in Matthew's Gospel where stuff is a problem. One stands out to me since it reads like a gloss on our passage in the Sermon on the Mount. Jesus has a chat with a fellow who asks him about eternal life (19:16-22), and eternal life suggests to me "treasures in heaven." Jesus responds by changing the subject and asking how he would "enter into life," the here and now, fully. Jesus instructs, "Keep the commandments." The fellow then begins to nickel and dime him (I thought that was a great metaphor, under the circumstances) by asking, "Which ones?" Jesus lists the second part of the Decalogue: no murder, no adultery, no stealing, no bearing false witness, honoring parents (Decalogue Part I), and he adds in "love your neighbor as yourself." If we look closely, we realize that one major commandment from the Decalogue goes missing: "You shall not covet . . . anything that belongs to your neighbor" (Exodus 20:17).

Not coveting was the one commandment this fellow, who "had many possessions" (Matthew 19:22), could not follow. That is, however, the one he needs to hear. Jesus tells him, "If you wish to be perfect, go, sell your possessions, and give the money to the poor, and you will have treasure in heaven; then come, follow me"

(v. 21). The fellow, grieving, does not accept the invitation. As he leaves, we hear the echo of the Sermon on the Mount: "Be perfect, therefore, as your heavenly Father is perfect" (5:48) and you will have "treasures in heaven" (6:20). The more the stuff, the further from perfection.

It is at this point that Jesus offers to his disciples the famous saying, "It is easier for a camel to go through the eye of a needle than for someone who is rich to enter the kingdom of God" (19:24). He is not saying that the rich, by definition, are damned, since "for God all things are possible" (v. 26). Nor is he alluding to some otherwise unknown camel gate, through which heavily laden camels enter but only after a bit of gymnastics. He is saying that those who store up treasures on earth will have proportionally fewer treasures in heaven. But those who know that life is more than stuff, who give rather than take, get a heavenly reward. More, they have peace on earth, for their heart is appropriately inclined not toward food, and not toward stuff, but toward God's will being done on earth as it is in heaven. And there, one finds one's treasure.

The Eye Is the Lamp of the Body

To find our treasure, we need to be aware that this treasure is not just something external: out there in the world or up there in the heavens. Our treasure is also part of us, who we are, in body and in spirit. Paul writes, "Do you not know that your body is a temple of the Holy Spirit within you, which you have from God" (1 Corinthians 6:19). Here in the Sermon on the Mount, the next two verses are about both actual bodies and how the body, specifically the eye, also has metaphorical meaning.

Jesus states, "The eye is the lamp of the body. So, if your eye is healthy, your whole body will be full of light; but if your eye is unhealthy, your whole body will be full of darkness. If then the light in you is darkness, how great is the darkness!" (Matthew 6:22-23). The relationship of the eye to the soul has become proverbial. To the Roman orator Cicero (106–43 BCE) is attributed the saying, "The face is a picture of the mind as the eyes are its interpreter."[1] More familiar is "the eyes are the windows to the soul." In seeking the origin of this phrase (it's not in the Bible, and it's not from Shakespeare), I came across lots of advertisements for liquid eyeliner along with the following quote, ascribed to Hiram Powers, an American sculptor: "The eye is the window of the soul, the mouth the door. The intellect, the will, are seen in the eye; the emotions, sensibilities, and affections, in the mouth. The animals look for man's intentions right into his eyes. Even a rat, when you hunt him and bring him to bay, looks you in the eye."[2]

It turns out that Jesus's comment about healthy eyes in relation to the rest of the body has medical backing. If the eye is cloudy, there's likely to be something wrong with the rest of the system; if we are happy, we tend to raise our eyebrows and so our eyes look bigger (hence the expression "bright-eyed"); when we smile, our eyes crinkle at the corners; our pupils respond by dilating or contracting in anticipation of a change in light or when we feel strong emotion. Speaking of the eyes thus marvelously fits within the Sermon, given its warnings against hypocrisy and egocentrism: most people can fake a smile, but we cannot control how our pupils respond. The eyes are less likely to be hypocritical (so much for the Eagles' song "Lyin' Eyes").

The reference to eyes also reflects back (that is the right metaphor) to Matthew 5:14, "You are the light of the world." Today, we know that receptors in the eye convert light into electrical signals that our brain then interprets: the light goes in. However, in antiquity, many people thought that the eye projected light out, hence the connection between eyes and lamps.

In antiquity, when people spoke of the "evil eye," they imagined that the evil eye would shoot out beams of malice. Today, children will sometimes talk about giving someone the "hairy eyeball," which is a third-grader's expression for looking at someone with malicious intent.

Putting 5:14 together with 6:22, we find the connection between proclamation and the ones who proclaim, the gospel and those who evangelize. The focus has shifted from fasting to eschewing externals, to the body. If an evil eye can cause malevolent reactions, then how much more can a good eye, an eye that conveys nothing but light, demonstrate how to find the "light of the world." It is inside those who follow the Sermon on the Mount, and it is also projected out by them.

The image of the eye as the lamp asks us, Are we looking through narrowed brows or bright eyes? Are we squinting and frowning, or do our eyes crinkle with delight? If we can set our eyes aright, then we can avoid that horrible hairy eyeball.

Jesus finally asks us to look and to attend to what we see. On what will our gaze alight? The question prepares us for the next section, where we look not to stuff that only we own, or stuff that we possess, but to the lilies and the ravens.

Do Not Worry

Comments about the eye being the lamp of the body should, literally, make us smile. Look for the crinkle in the corner of your eye: that will help determine if the smile is sincere or forced. But if you are smiling because you're doing a study of the Sermon on the Mount, then of course: how better to be the light of the world.

That smile helps as we come to the end of Matthew 6. Here the imperatives become, in our increasingly troubled world, impossible, or laughable. Jesus begins, "Therefore [the Greek says "Amen"] I tell you, do not worry about your life, what you will eat or what you will drink, or about your body, what you will wear. Is not life more than food, and the body more than clothing?" (v. 25). The eye is the lamp of the body: Upon what do those metaphorical lights coming from the eyes shine?

Jesus, appropriately, begins with what he has advised the disciples give up: stuff. The rabbinic tradition agrees with him: Avot 2:7

notes, "lots of property, lots of worries." Anyone who has the ability to fast—which means anyone who has food that can go uneaten—already does not worry about food and drink. We have it. Since our eyes are good, we don't have to worry about our bodies; that internal light is already shining outward. He's already told us that life is more than food, for "one does not live by bread alone." He's already told us that our bodies, in the image and likeness of the divine, are splendidly made: "your whole body will be full of light" if you find your treasure, and so your heart (Matthew 6:22).

Paul, like Jesus, gives the Gentiles in his assemblies the same advice: "Do not worry about anything, but in everything by prayer and supplication with thanksgiving let your requests be made known to God. And the peace of God, which surpasses all understanding, will guard your hearts and your minds in Christ Jesus" (Philippians 4:6-7). At the time he wrote Philippians, Paul was in prison and likely knew he would die. Nevertheless, he models for his readers what he himself believes: "I know what it is to have little, and I know what it is to have plenty. In any and all circumstances I have learned the secret of being well-fed and of going hungry, of having plenty and of being in need. I can do all things through him who strengthens me" (vv. 12-13).

If Paul, in prison, knows that prayer and thanksgiving create peace, then worry is not the problem. For Jesus's disciples, and for Matthew's community, there's no reason to worry. These are people committed to sharing their daily bread—and these will be people who mark their gatherings by a meal that recalls how Jesus, at his final supper, shared his bread and wine (Matthew 26:26-28). Bread and wine and so much more.

Jesus then trains their eyes on the natural world and away from what we make with our hands:

> "Look at the birds of the air; they neither sow nor reap nor gather into barns, and yet your heavenly Father feeds them. Are you not of more value than they? And can any of you by worrying add a single hour to your span of life? And why

do you worry about clothing? Consider the lilies of the field, how they grow; they neither toil nor spin, yet I tell you, even Solomon in all his glory was not clothed like one of these. But if God so clothes the grass of the field, which is alive today and tomorrow is thrown into the oven, will he not much more clothe you—you of little faith?" (6:26-30).

The image he evokes is an idealized one: with pollution and drought, birds do not always sing, and flowers do not always gloriously bloom. Yet the verdant fields of the Galilee may well have looked that day, as Jesus spoke, as if they were a gift from God. Because we in the twenty-first century know of ecological disasters, Jesus's first words, "Look at the birds of the air. . . . Consider the lilies of the field," mean we must attend to nature. The birds and the flowers are not merely examples of good gifts; they are our responsibility since to humanity God gave "dominion over the fish of the sea and over the birds of the air and over every living thing that moves upon the earth. . . . I have given you every plant yielding seed that is upon the face of all the earth, and every tree with seed in its fruit; you shall have them for food" (Genesis 1:28-29).

Jesus is not saying we should be like the birds or the lilies: our jobs include the sowing, the reaping, the harvesting, the textile manufacturing, and so on. But we can learn from the simplicity and the ephemerality of their lives. Not only can we "look," we can also "consider." We can learn.

In fact, if we consider closely, we may find an inside joke. Luke's version of these sayings reads, "Consider the ravens: they neither sow nor reap, they have neither storehouse nor barn, and yet God feeds them. Of how much more value are you than the birds!" (12:24). Ironically, it is ravens that feed the prophet Elijah (1 Kings 17).

The disciples learn from the birds and the lilies that they need not worry about food or clothes, for God provides for them: "Therefore do not worry, saying, 'What will we eat?' or 'What will we drink?' or 'What will we wear?' For it is the Gentiles who strive for all these things; and indeed your heavenly Father knows that you need all these things. But strive first for the kingdom of God and his righteousness, and all these things will be given to you as well" (Matthew 6:31-33).

Now we trace the import of the verses. The disciples learn from Torah, from lilies and ravens, from Jesus, and from one another. They are not part of the wider Gentile world that lives by the standards of the Roman Empire; they are disciples who live in a group that shares bread and forgives debt; they are part of a group that seeks peaceful resolutions rather than judicial or military conflict. Now the earlier comment from the Sermon—"and if anyone wants to sue you and take your coat, give your cloak as well" (5:40)—takes on heightened meaning: don't worry about your clothes.

The disciples shortly will learn that they will be judged on how they fed and clothed others: "For I was hungry and you gave me food, I was thirsty and you gave me something to drink. . . . I was naked and you gave me clothing" (25:35-36). Indeed, the Passion narrative offers juxtaposed verses that show, with exquisite irony, why one need not worry about food and clothing: "They offered him wine to drink, mixed with gall; but when he tasted it, he would not drink it. And when they had crucified him, they divided his clothes among themselves by casting lots" (27:34-35).

The few verses teach us even more. Jesus is telling his disciples not to worry about what gets put on the table or about designer labels and last year's fashion. In this community, heaven forbid that one is judged by food or clothing, which means being judged by how much money one has to spend for the goods, how much leisure time one has to cook or to sew, or how much surplus one has to pay others to perform these labors. The Epistle of James, which has multiple connections to the Sermon on the Mount, addresses this issue directly:

> Do you with your acts of favoritism really believe in our glorious Lord Jesus Christ? For if a person with gold rings and in fine clothes comes into your assembly [*synagogue*],

and if a poor person in dirty clothes also comes in, and if you take notice of the one wearing the fine clothes and say, "Have a seat here, please," while to the one who is poor you say, "Stand there," or, "Sit at my feet," have you not made distinctions among yourselves, and become judges with evil thoughts? (2:1-4)

Treasure cannot be found in food, for it will go stale if not consumed, and if it is consumed, well, we know where that ends up. And treasure cannot be found in clothing, for this year's fashion is next year's folly. One finds one's treasure elsewhere.

Do Not Worry—Really

Matthew chapter 6 ends with a summary of the several previous verses: "But strive first for the kingdom of God and his righteousness, and all these things will be given to you as well. So do not worry about tomorrow, for tomorrow will bring worries of its own" (vv. 33-34). At this point, I have an image of the disciples looking at Jesus with a combination of confusion and horror. A few are thinking *Not worry? Are you nuts?* James are John are worried about their mom and dad, Peter about his mother-in-law (and, I hope, his wife). Jesus looks at their faces, especially at their narrowed if not tear-filled eyes, and says, "Listen, don't worry about tomorrow. You've got enough problems for today. Just deal with that." They'll only learn the truth of his words once the mission gets underway (after all, it's only chapter 6 of 28).

I've had some students who worry about worrying, and when they worry, they fear they have sinned: "I have an exam tomorrow, and I'm worried—so now I can't study because since I'm worried I'm sinful, and I need to pray." It's an interesting rationale for being unprepared. My advice to them is that worry will not help them; study will. And then I paraphrase Jesus, "If you've striven first for the kingdom of God and his righteousness, and you've done the reading, you'll be fine."

Postscript: OK, I'm going to worry anyway. I think worrying is in my DNA. My mother worried; her mother worried; all the way back to Mount Sinai, the women in my family worried. But we all had coping mechanisms. Turns out, they are pretty much the same thing Jesus advises. If you are prepared, which means you have your priorities in order—that "you strive first for the kingdom of God and his righteousness"—then you have no need to worry. Indeed, you have no need to "worry about how you are to speak or what you are to say" (10:19), for you, by the power both of the Spirit and of your own dedicated work, will be fine.

Do Not Judge

Finding one's treasure consists of both attitude and action, looking outward and introspection, the alignment of the body and the spirit. It's a process, but like muscle memory, living into the kingdom does become easier with intention and practice. Having prepared his disciples physically and mentally, Jesus now admonishes them, "Do not judge, so that you may not be judged. For with the judgment you make you will be judged, and the measure you give will be the measure you get" (7:1-2). No anger, no lust, no worry, and now no judging: he asks a lot. And why not? He's continuing to set a high bar, just as Torah sets a high bar. I would expect no less.

Jesus backs up his admonition in terms of reciprocity, a teaching technique he has already used on the Sermon, as in, "And forgive us our debts, as we also have forgiven our debtors" (6:12). Here he states that the criteria we use to judge others will be used to judge us, and that is the last thing many of us want.

He is *not* saying that we should become bystanders or that we should not seek justice. We are not to think, when seeing a wrong being committed, *It's not my job to judge, so I'm just going to let it happen.* To the contrary: Torah insists, "You shall not hate in your heart anyone of your kin; you shall reprove your neighbor, or you will incur guilt yourself" (Leviticus 19:17). You cannot rebuke if you are unable to judge right from wrong. Moreover, we see in this verse from Leviticus the same sort of reciprocity Jesus invokes in the Sermon on the Mount. Finding one's treasure always has a relational, or communitarian, aspect. It cannot be done alone.

He is also *not* saying that we should park our ability to discern the good from the bad at the baptismal font. Discernment is essential. "Do not judge" does not mean abdicating one's responsibility for preventing harm.

One way of reframing his statement is to move from "do not judge" to "do not be judgmental, fault-finding, hypercritical." Therefore, "do not judge" means do not put yourself in the role of God; it does mean: do not presume to know what's in someone's heart. Paul offers a variant of this teaching in his Epistle to the Romans, for he knows that some members of the congregation are negatively judging others who have different practices. He starts in Romans 2:1 by telling these judgmental individuals, "Therefore you have no excuse, whoever you are, when you judge others; for in passing judgment on another you condemn yourself, because you, the judge, are doing the very same things." In chapter 14, he returns to this theme:

> Who are you to [judge] servants of another? It is before their own lord that they stand or fall. And they will be upheld, for the Lord is able to make them stand. . . . Why do you [judge] your brother or sister? Or you, why do you despise your brother or sister? For we will all stand before the judgment seat of God. . . . Let us therefore no longer [judge] one another, but resolve instead never to put a stumbling block or hindrance in the way of another. (vv. 4, 10, 13)

The import of these verses came home powerfully to me when I began to teach at Riverbend Maximum Security Institution, a maximum-security prison in Nashville. My students there always remind me, and the Vanderbilt students in class with them, that their crime is not the sum total of who they are. As if they were channeling Jesus, they ask, "Would you want to be judged by, or even known by, the worst thing you've ever done in your life?"

When it comes to judging, especially in terms of a person's morality or the total of their deeds, that is not our call. That is, according to Matthew, the role of the Son of Man, who "comes in his glory, and all the angels with him, then he will sit on the throne of his glory. All the nations will be gathered before him, and he will separate people one from another as a shepherd separates the sheep from the goats" (25:31-32).

Another form of judging that has become increasingly prominent in today's society is that of judging people in the past by the standards of the present. For example, many of my students are appalled by the Bible's acceptance of slavery, and a few think the entire text should be consigned to the trash heap. At the same time, it was the Bible that motivated the abolitionists and fueled antislavery movements. The history of how Christians came to reject slavery is a fascinating study of how biblical interpretation has changed over the centuries. The interpretive models we have now—better translations of the Greek; better knowledge of Jesus's Jewish context; moving away from literalism to concerns for sociology and psychology; considering different perspectives from people of different social locations—help determine how we understand a text. We might wonder how, a century from now, our descendants will judge us. Will people condemn me because I live in a single-dwelling home rather than in an intentional community where residents share a common kitchen and eat only what they grow themselves? I don't know.

Rather than judging others for the purpose of condemnation, we are better off attending to our own blind spots. Jesus, returning to the image of the eye, asks, "Why do you see the speck in your neighbor's eye, but do not notice the log in your own eye? Or how can you say to your neighbor, 'Let me take the speck out of your eye,' while the log is in your own eye?" He then answers his own question: "You hypocrite, first take the log out of your own eye, and then you will see clearly to take the speck out of your neighbor's eye" (7:3-5). The eye cannot be the lamp of the body if it's got specks in it; the disciple cannot be the light of the world if that disciple is too busy judging the world rather than healing its brokenness.

Finding the treasure sometimes requires withholding the easy judgmentalism to which we are all tempted. It means offering constructive rather than destructive criticism when criticism is needed. It means discerning when to speak and when to be silent; it means bringing light to the situation rather than heat.

Chapter 6

LIVING INTO THE KINGDOM

The beginning of the Sermon on the Mount establishes the kingdom's priorities: righteousness and servant leadership, practicing as well as praying and preaching, creating not just a community but a family, avoiding hypocrisy, both creating peace with others and finding peace in ourselves. The Sermon now, in Matthew 7:6-27, concludes with a combination of assurance for the future and guidelines for the present.

As with the previous chapters, books could be written about each verse, for each image recalls or anticipates other images in the Gospel, finds connections to passages in the Scriptures of Israel (what will be the Old Testament), and speaks not only to an ancient audience but also to any concerned about living into the kingdom of heaven by helping to create it on earth.

Pearls Before Swine

Sometimes advice sounds so obvious that we wonder why it needs to be offered at all. "Do not give what is holy to dogs; and do not throw your pearls before swine, or they will trample them under foot and turn and maul you" (7:6). I have never been tempted to throw my pearls before swine, or any other animal for that matter. Nor have I felt the urge to give what I consider holy to dogs, despite the fact that I have an adorable puppy (and that the puppy would be inclined to eat whatever is holy, and anything else, is another matter). Consequently, we need to determine why Jesus would issue such a statement, and the answer has to be something better than, "after demanding love of enemies, commending extraordinary generosity, and advising, 'Don't worry,' it's about time we got a verse that we can follow without too much effort."

To get an answer, we first need to clean out one incorrect teaching that has become popular in a number of churches. Despite claims by numerous sermons, "dogs" does *not* mean "Gentiles"; Jews did not typically call Gentiles dogs. Nor did Jews, in general, find dogs to be unclean or disgusting animals. To the contrary, the Book of Tobit remarks that the hero Tobias is accompanied by a dog (Tobit 6:2; 11:4).

Readers get the idea that Jews called Gentiles dogs from another passage in Matthew where Jesus refers to a Canaanite woman, desperate for him to perform an exorcism on her demon-possessed daughter, as a dog. When she begs for his help, he responds, "It is not fair to take the children's food and throw it to the dogs" (Matthew 15:26; compare Mark 7:27). The term *dog* (Greek: *kynarion*) really means "little dogs" or "puppies." Granted, it's still an insult, but the impression is of household pet rather than mangy scavenger. In the Hebrew Bible and in rabbinic sources, the term *dog* has no connotation of "Gentile." The term *dog* was a standard ancient insult found in the works of Aristotle, Euripides, Quintilian, and other Greek and Latin writers.

The Canaanite woman responds by accepting the insult and then turning Jesus's image back on him: "Yes, Lord, yet even the dogs eat the crumbs that fall from their masters' table" (v. 27). There could not be a more brilliant enacting of the Sermon on the Mount. Along with turning the other cheek, giving the coat, and going the extra mile, the Canaanite woman offers accepting the insult but holding fast to her righteous case. She does not return insult for insult; she does not exacerbate the violence. Instead, she keeps the channels of communication open; she works with what Jesus has given her.

Much more could be said about this story: the relationship of Israelites to Canaanites; the differing details between Mark's account of a Syrophoenician woman with a demon-possessed daughter and Matthew's Canaanite woman with the same urgent problem; the role of the disciples in Matthew's version; the importance of the distinct settings of each story; how the story speaks to both those with resources (the powerful) and those in need (the ones with less power), and so on. For our purposes, we know that when we come to this difficult encounter in Matthew 15 Jesus has spoken about not throwing what is holy to dogs. And we learn from this connection that the supplicant is *no dog*. No supplicant is. Therefore, in relation to mission or evangelism, disciples should never think of outsiders as less than human.

More, the juxtaposition of the Sermon on the Mount with the story of the Canaanite woman reinforces the fact that we can, in prayer, express what we need to the point of making demands on God. Just as disciples pray "give us this day . . . forgive us our debts," so they can continue to make demands, as the woman says, "Have mercy on me, Lord, Son of David. . . . Help me" (Matthew 15:22, 25).

The verse finds another connection in Matthew's Gospel: the parable of the pearl of great price (13:45-46).[1] The pearl, so precious to the merchant, should never be given away, let alone to those who have no interest in appreciating it. Something so precious is not to be wasted.

Although the disciples are to be a light to the nations, they are also to manage their resources. The comment about pearls before swine comes immediately after Jesus's warning against judgmentalism. Thus he reinforces the point that the issue regarding judging is not assessing resource allocation but fault finding. Now Jesus tells his disciples that they should take care both in their proclamations and in their allocations not to put themselves in danger, lest "they

will trample [the good gifts] under foot and turn and maul you"
(7:6). Disciples are to be generous and compassionate; they are not
to be stupid.

Knock, and the Door Will Be Opened for You

Jesus states, "Ask, and it will be given you; search, and you
will find; knock, and the door will be opened for you. For everyone
who asks receives, and everyone who searches finds, and for everyone who knocks, the door will be opened" (Matthew 7:7-8). We
have here another "Really, Jesus?" moment, as anyone who has ever
canvassed for a candidate, accompanied a child selling Girl Scout
cookies, or sought to bring the gospel to the neighborhood knows:
not all doors open. Indeed, even in the Gospel, not all doors open.
In the parable of the wise and foolish virgins, the five foolish—
having gone to the local 7-Eleven to purchase oil—find the door
to the wedding feast closed. They call out, "'Lord, lord, open to
us.'" The answer they receive is harsh: "'Amen [NRSV: truly] I tell
you, I do not know you.'" The parable concludes with the warning,
"Keep awake therefore, for you know neither the day nor the hour"
(25:11-13).

With this intertext, we can now respond to those canvassers
and guardians and evangelists who could not get a foot in the door.
They have the wrong interpretation of this knocking and this door.
We recall that Jesus is talking to his disciples about the community
to be founded in his name. He's not talking about strangers; he's
talking about people in the group, the new family with one foot in
the kingdom of heaven. If the disciple has need, the disciple knows
that the door will be open, what is needed will be found, what is
asked will be answered.

While community members are to be a light to the world, and
they are to give when asked, they will still have in their minds the
admonition of the previous verse. They are to help the disadvan-
taged, not to be taken advantage of. Again, one can be generous

without being stupid. Disciples are called to be the light of the world, not dim bulbs.

Ask and knock also mean, in terms of human relations, don't demand and don't barge in. There's a civility to the community the Sermon on the Mount envisions, a civility frequently missing in the kingdoms on earth. At the same time, there is a boldness that the community members possess: they can express their needs to others, who will answer; the homeless will find a home, and the hungry will find food. More, they do well to choose carefully the door at which they will knock. They knock at the door of the family.

Jesus makes this point clear in the next two lines, which turn to familial images: "Is there anyone among you who, if your child asks for bread, will give a stone? Or if the child asks for a fish, will give a snake?" (7:9-10). Our answer to Jesus's rhetorical question is, initially, "of course not." But on second thought, we know better. Not all parents are responsible, and the verse gives the Bible study leader the opportunity to raise important questions of abuse or neglect. In the kingdom of heaven, all children are fed and loved. In the kingdom of heaven, all adults are responsible and loving. These verses about asking, seeking, and knocking also return us to the Beatitudes. If you're mourning, you will be comforted. If you are in need of compassion, compassion will be shown to you.

References to bread and fish find their own connections in Matthew's Gospel and beyond. The term *bread* is used three hundred times in the New Revised Standard Version of the Bible; some will provide better nuances to our verse than others. Bread references so permeate Matthew's Gospel that the text comes to smell like a bakery. We started with the temptation narrative, where Satan demanded of Jesus to turn stones into bread (4:3). Now we have a different command: the child who demands to be fed. While Jesus responded to Satan that we do not "live by bread alone," here we realize how necessary actual bread, actual food, is to life.

Next, disciples should identify not only with the kind parent but also with the child who demands bread, since they have been taught to pray for daily bread (6:11). We can go to all the other bread references in Matthew: the "bread of the Presence" in 12:4, the feeding of the five thousand in chapter 16, the metaphoric use of leaven to refer to evil in 16:5-12, the Passover, the holiday of the Unleavened Bread (26:17), and the Eucharist of 26:26. All the spiritual meaning, intertextual allusions, and literary brilliance of these verses pales in the face of a hungry child.

Nor should that fish image be allowed to swim away. At the end of the Gospel of John, the evangelist offers one more miraculous event. The disciples have been fishing, and suddenly the resurrected Jesus appears. Following the astonishing haul, Jesus invites them, "Come and have breakfast." He then "took the bread and gave it to them, and did the same with the fish" (21:12-13). That child in the Sermon on the Mount is asking for bread and fish, and more: that child is asking to share a meal with the resurrected Christ and his other followers.

As God acts, so humanity is to act. And as those with one foot in the kingdom act, so in turn God acts, since the relationship between heaven and earth is reciprocal. Jesus concludes this section of the Sermon by observing, "If you then, who are evil, know how to give good gifts to your children, how much more will your Father in heaven give good things to those who ask him!" (Matthew 7:11). That exclamation point is not in any early Greek manuscript, but it strikes me as appropriate here.

When the community does the divine will, then the community is in the image of the divine. And it is part of divine will to open the door to those who seek to enter. A medieval Rosh Hashanah (New Year's Day) prayer book describes God as one "who opens the door to those who knock in repentance. And all believe that His hand is open; Who eagerly waits for the wicked [to repent], and desires his justification. And all believe that He is just and upright."[2] If we ask God for forgiveness, that door will open.

Less obvious is the opening comment, "If you then, who are evil" (Matthew 7:11; compare Luke 11:13). Wait! Evil? Who? Us? Some conservative commentators use this verse to support the idea of humanity's total depravity. Personally, I don't feel totally depraved, and personally, I don't think humanity is totally depraved either. Other commentators suggest that "evil" here means "sinful," but that also seems off topic. More, Jesus knows the word for sinful, but that's not the term used in Matthew 7:11. Behind the translation "evil" is the Greek *poneros*, the same term we find in the Our Father prayer's "deliver us from the evil one."

Jesus is not saying that humanity is the equivalent of Satan. Nor do I think he is suggesting that we are totally depraved. That would be odd, given that he's just informed his disciples that they are the salt of the earth and the light of the world and that they are blessed.

There are at least three better readings than the condemnation of the entire human condition (and I suspect readers can find more). First, resisting reaction is appropriate: "I am not evil; I am not Satan." Thus, we recognize that we are already aware that we are basically good people, and at the same time we are aware that, given the imperatives in the Sermon on the Mount, we can do better. Second, compared to God, everyone is evil; that's how high the standard is that Jesus sets. There's a Gospel verse that Mark (10:18) and Luke (18:19) record, but Matthew does not. Jesus is speaking to the rich man who refused to become his disciple because he could not part with his stuff. The man addresses Jesus as "Good teacher," and Jesus responds, "Why do you call me good? No one is good but God alone."

Third, Jesus offers an argument familiar from rabbinic literature. Called *qal v'homer*, literally "light and heavy," the formulation is "If X, then how much more so Y?" For example, as Jesus says, "Suppose one of you has only one sheep and it falls into a pit on the sabbath; will you not lay hold of it and lift it out? How much more valuable is a human being than a sheep! So it is lawful to do good on the sabbath" (Matthew 12:11-12). If X (you help a sheep), then how much more so Y (you should help a human being)?

Now we can find another meaning to our verse: if we who are not perfect—we who are sometimes selfish and vain, resentful and lazy—can meet our children's needs, indeed, we can "give good gifts to [our] children, how much more will [the] Father in Heaven give good things to those who ask" (7:11). The title for God then recalls the gifts: daily bread, forgiveness, providing guidance, delivering from the very evil that surrounds us and sometimes infects us.

Do to Others

The Golden Rule is, in various forms, found across the globe, and its benefits are well known. Less familiar is the line that follows it in the Gospel: "for this is the law and the prophets." By Law and Prophets (my capitalizations are deliberate), Jesus is referring to the Torah (the Pentateuch) and the Prophets (former and latter). At the time of Jesus, the third part of the Jewish canon, the Writings, was still in flux (for example, the Book of Esther has never been found among the Dead Sea Scrolls). Jesus thus summarizes the Scriptures of Israel by the Golden Rule.

That is not his only summary. When a lawyer (in Matthew; a scribe in Mark) asks him "which commandment in the law is the greatest?" Jesus responds, "'You shall love the Lord your God with all your heart, and with all your soul, and with all your mind,'" and, "'You shall love your neighbor as yourself.'" He concludes, "On these two commandments hang all the law and the prophets" (Matthew 22:35-40). Thus, the Scriptures of Israel can be summarized in two ways: the Golden Rule and Love of God/Love of Neighbor.

But a summary is not sufficient; the summary is the guide through which the rest of Torah, and Jesus's teachings, should be filtered. Jesus himself cites other commandments that he expects his disciples to follow, including in the extensions of the Sermon on the Mount. Without the full biblical context—especially the Gospel's interest in higher righteousness, loving enemies, and avoiding hypocrisy—the Golden Rule is easily deformed. A missionary might think, *Because I would want to be a Christian and would, therefore, want to be disabused of my previous, non-Christian culture, therefore I will not only take indigenous children away from their parents but also forbid them from speaking their own language and worshipping their own gods.* In evangelizing—in being the light of the world and to the world—one does well to show what is right with one's own tradition, not what is wrong with someone else's. One evangelizes by love, not by compulsion.

There's an alternative version of the Golden Rule called the Silver Rule—and so perceived to be of slightly less value. In the context of instruction to his son Tobias, Tobit advises, inter alia, "Do not keep over until the next day the wages of those who work for you, but pay them at once. If you serve God you will receive payment. Watch yourself, my son, in everything you do, and discipline yourself in all your conduct. And what you hate, do not do to anyone. Do not drink wine to excess or let drunkenness go with you on your way" (Tobit 4:14-15). For Tobit, the Silver Rule is proverbial wisdom.

Recall the story from the introduction of Hillel for another iteration of the rule. When a Gentile demanded, "Convert me on condition that you teach me the entire Torah while I am standing on one foot," Hillel responded, "That which is hateful to you do not do to another; that is the entire Torah, and the rest is its interpretation. Go study" (Shabbat 31a).

The Silver Rule, if taken out of its Jewish context, can also be deformed. "Don't do to others" can be an excuse for inaction. But in its context, we know that it is a touchstone, or a canon within a canon, by which all the other *mitzvot* (commandments) should be understood. In these various iterations—by Jesus, Tobit, and

Hillel—the rule never stands alone; it is always accompanied by and understood in the context of the rest of Scripture.

The Narrow Gate

The Law and Prophets can be summarized and serve as a touchstone by which we interpret the other commandments and teachings. In effect, the summaries provide one reading of the "narrow gate" to which Jesus now turns: "Enter through the narrow gate; for the gate is wide and the road is easy that leads to destruction, and there are many who take it. For the gate is narrow and the road is hard that leads to life, and there are few who find it" (Matthew 7:13-14; compare Luke 13:23-24).

The warning against taking the easy path is a reiteration of "do not bring us to the test" or "lead us not into temptation." The easy path tempts: it is easier to hate one's enemies than to love them; it is easier to sue someone than to work toward reconciliation; it is easier to be judgmental than to be humble, and so on.

Juxtaposed to the Golden Rule and the reference to Torah and Prophets, the verse takes on heightened meaning: when you interpret Scripture, don't take the easy route of yanking a verse out of context (for example, verses that cause churches to schism)—especially if it speaks to your own political views; take the narrow route of filtering it through the love command.

Although the Sermon on the Mount begins with the Beatitudes and the promises of comfort, it moves inexorably to challenges to that comfort. Jesus is not selling his disciples a false hope; he is excruciatingly honest with them. In this same Gospel, he will tell these same disciples, and anyone else who claims that designation, "whoever does not take up the cross and follow me is not worthy of me" (Matthew 10:38) and "if any want to become my followers, let them deny themselves and take up their cross and follow me" (Matthew 16:24). The cross is the narrow way. It is also the way to show love. No one said the path into the kingdom would be easy.

But is it worthwhile? Absolutely, because it allows disciples to focus their love and their talents, to have better knowledge of self and better concepts of living within a community.

Discerning False Prophets and Bearing Good Fruit

False prophets tend to be those who proclaim the wide gate and the easy road, or better, "easy street." They might look pious in their "sheep's clothing," while they are anything but. Their clothing, their trappings, signal that they are members of the community gathered in Jesus's name; their actions say otherwise. False prophets tend to preach but not practice. They may ask you for your money, but the funds go to their private jets rather than to health care or housing. They proclaim a constricted form of morality and then engage in their own sexual escapades.

False prophets are also those who say "Lord Lord"—and that's it. To say "all you need to do is believe in Jesus and you will be saved" is to deform the gospel; to say "the narrow gate means confessing Jesus as Lord" mistakes the notice that after one goes through the gate, one enters the "hard" (that is, difficult) road that leads to life (Matthew 7:13-14).

The false prophet has apparently missed the entire Sermon on the Mount, Jesus's teachings about the cross, the parable of the sheep and the goats, and pretty much all of the Bible.

Jesus makes clear how one knows a false prophet: he doesn't have to be a prophet himself, for here the teaching is obvious, "You will know them by their fruits" (7:16, 20). Paul makes a similar point: "The fruit of the Spirit is love, joy, peace, patience, kindness, generosity, faithfulness, gentleness, and self-control" (Galatians 5:22-23). Our problem, and the problem people in Jesus's day also had, is that the good fruit is not always obvious. Then, and now, people are swayed by false prophets who substitute charisma for good works and promises for concrete action. Matthew later defines these "false prophets" as well as "false messiahs": they are the ones who "produce great signs and omens, to lead astray, if possible, even the elect" (24:24 and see 24:11).

Later in the Sermon on the Mount, Jesus speaks of those false prophets who, at the final judgment, say, "Lord, Lord, did we not prophesy in your name, and cast out demons in your name, and do many deeds of power in your name?" Jesus will respond: "I never knew you; go away from me, you evildoers" (7:22-23). The NRSV here does not quite get the correct nuance. The Greek beneath "evildoers" is "[people] working lawlessness." The reference to law and so to Torah thus frames the Sermon. Jesus begins with the assertion that he has not come to abolish Torah and Prophets; he ends the Sermon by condemning those people, *in his community*, who would deny those very teachings.

We see similar problems with false prophets throughout the biblical tradition. Deuteronomy 18:20 warns of a "prophet who speaks in the name of other gods"—an ancient verse that finds purchase today in the prophets of the quick fix, the magic diet, and the "pass the class without studying" (the one I particularly abhor). Paul is concerned with the "super-apostles" who have glorious rhetoric but proclaim a message different than his (2 Corinthians 11:5); 1 John 4:1-2 advises, "Do not believe every spirit, but test the spirits to see whether they are from God; for many false prophets have gone out into the world. By this you know the Spirit of God: every spirit that confesses that Jesus Christ has come in the flesh is from God"; and 2 Peter 2:1 notes, "false prophets also arose among the people, just as there will be false teachers among you, who will secretly bring in destructive opinions." False prophets have continued to arise through the centuries with their false promises.

Discernment should be based not by these prophets' theology, not by politics, and not by what church they attend: discernment is based on what they do. The point applies to individuals, and it applies to churches as well. When the service becomes a show designed to entertain rather than to comfort and encourage, when people attend more because of cultural pressure than need for community, when genuine curiosity about the Bible is closed down rather than encouraged, false prophets are lurking.

Leave the walking on water to Jesus; instead, feed the hungry. Leave the signs and wonders to the prophets of Israel and John the Baptist; instead, clothe the naked. Leave the deeds of power, the "mighty works," to God; instead, welcome the stranger. To do that is miracle enough.

Jesus correctly notes that "a good tree cannot bear bad fruit, nor can a bad tree bear good fruit" (Matthew 7:18). I originally thought he was being predestinarian: some people are born good and others born evil. I was wrong. Talking about this verse, one of my students at Riverbend Maximum Security Institution said, "I was a bad tree—producing fruit of drug dealing and pimping. No more." He had good biblical backing. Whereas in Matthew, Jesus next says, "Every tree that does not bear good fruit is cut down and thrown into the fire" (7:19), a parable in Luke's Gospel offers a different perspective.

According to this less well-known parable,

> A man had a fig tree planted in his vineyard; and he came looking for fruit on it and found none. So he said to the gardener, "See here! For three years I have come looking for fruit on this fig tree, and still I find none. Cut it down! Why should it be wasting the soil?" He replied, "Sir, let it alone for one more year, until I dig around it and put manure on it. If it bears fruit next year, well and good; but if not, you can cut it down." (13:6-9)

Everyone gets a second chance, especially in places where both communal forgiveness and communal concern for responsibility are present. A little fertilizer can go a long way. A little patience can as well.

That chance, finally, is not determined by theological confession. It is determined by action, perhaps action that flows from that confession. Matthew's concern is not the dreaded "works righteousness"; Matthew's concern is people who do not bear good fruit.

Those Who Say "Lord, Lord"

The Sermon, which began with such comfort in the Beatitudes, now ends with the challenge of warning. Matthew knows of those false prophets who promised a good life but delivered smoke and mirrors; Matthew also knows of people who continually express their faith in Jesus, but their fruits are lacking. There's a popular sermon illustration of the police officer who pulls over a car adorned with bumper stickers: "Follow me to Church," "My boss is a Jewish carpenter," "Honk if you love Jesus," "Driverless car in case of Rapture," "Smile, Jesus loves you," "Not perfect, just forgiven," and so on. The driver is confused: "Officer, what did I do wrong?" The officer responds, "You honked at the old lady in the crosswalk, signaled with your middle finger to the Toyota that passed you, and screamed an obscenity at the car ahead of you at the stoplight—I figured, given your bumper stickers, that the car was stolen."

Confession is insufficient. Church attendance is insufficient. Memorization of the Bible is insufficient (although I grant it is impressive). "Only the one who does the will of my Father in heaven" (Matthew 7:21), says Jesus, will enter. That will is the Torah, understood through Jesus's teaching in the Sermon on the Mount, and that will is the Sermon on the Mount, understood through the rest of the Gospel.

With this understanding, one has the firm foundation, the "house on rock" that can withstand any temptation (7:24). The firm foundation requires time, and it requires action. A firm foundation cannot be in the mind only; it is built with the action of hands and feet. As the Epistle of James so eloquently puts it, "Faith without works is . . . dead" (2:26). If we missed the point in the Sermon on the Mount, the rest of the Gospel will remind us.

Combining the tree image and the house image is a lovely passage from *Pirke Avot*, which we recall is, comparable to the Sermon the Mount, the collected sayings of a number of rabbis. Avot 3:17 offers,

> Anyone whose wisdom is greater than his deeds—to what is he to be likened? To a tree with abundant foliage, but few roots. When the winds come, they will uproot it and blow it down, as it is said, *"He shall be like a tamarisk in the desert and shall not see when good comes but shall inhabit the parched places in the wilderness"* [Jeremiah 17:6]. But anyone whose deeds are greater than his wisdom—to what is he to be likened? To a tree with little foliage but abundant roots. For even if all the winds in the world were to come and blast at it, they will not move it from its place, as it is said, *"He shall be as a tree planted by the waters, and that spreads out its roots by the river, and shall not fear when heat comes, and his leaf shall be green, and shall not be careful in the year of drought, neither shall cease from yielding fruit"* (Jeremiah 17:8).

The abundant foliage is for show—looks good, offers little. The deep roots, the firm foundation, derive from knowing the scriptural teachings and acting on them.

Teaching with Authority

When Jesus finished all these things, those listening in were astounded, for he taught them as one having authority and not like their scribes. The scribes have their own understanding of Torah, which they developed in community of other scribes. Similarly, the people who wrote the Dead Sea Scrolls, Philo the Jewish philosopher from Alexandria, Hillel and Shammai, and others had their own take. Jesus has his. Unlike the scribes, he does not cite the teachings of a particular school of thought; nor does he argue many of his points. He speaks with authority: not granted by his teachers, not granted by a community that went to the Dead Sea, not granted by years of study.

We know what the crowds thought. We might wonder what the disciples were thinking, but we know that they continued to follow him, and some would die for him. For they heard in his teachings the path toward the kingdom of heaven, and they will see in his actions how to enter that narrow gate.

Afterword

THE KINGDOM AMONG AND WITHIN

For Jesus, life meant being part of a community. His comment in Luke 17:21, "The kingdom of God is among you," demonstrates that communal presence. When people take seriously the Sermon on the Mount—when they conquer their anger, when they love not only their neighbors but also their enemies—the kingdom is present. We can also extend that comment from Luke's Gospel to find a type of internal kingdom, one that is not only communal but also individual. When we practice our piety not for accolades, when we find our treasure by focusing on what is of ultimate import, then the kingdom becomes incarnated inside of us. Both we and the world in which we live become transformed.

It is impossible to sustain the sense of the kingdom's presence. Stuff gets in the way. Life gets in the way. Failing bodies get in the way. We can't be perfect all the time. These moments of doubt, frustration, jealousy, greed, or despair are not failures or disappointments; they are opportunities. Our heavenly treasure is still safely deposited in that heavenly treasure box, even if it seems like we can't find the key. Neither Judaism nor Christianity is a finished project; both traditions are looking forward to that messianic age where there is real peace on earth and real peace in the human heart. When we lose the presence of the kingdom, Jesus offers exactly the right petition: "Your kingdom come" means that, although it is not here yet, we can do more than simply pray for it. We can demand it of the divine (that verse is in the imperative), and then we can go out and bear the fruits that will bring it back into our lives and our hearts.

There are many first steps for entering the kingdom, since despite the communal emphasis, each person has distinct talents and distinct needs. Any verse in the Sermon on the Mount can provide an entry. I believe the same can be said for other texts held sacred by other traditions. For the path the Sermon on the Mount presents, we start with the good news of the Beatitudes. We know that our yearning for righteousness, our refusal to use our privilege for our own benefit, our mourning—all of these responses to the demands the world puts on us—have value. The Beatitudes tell us that we—each of us individually—are not the center of the world. Nor do we need to be. We are not its center; we are its light and salt.

The Sermon reinforces another path when Jesus affirms the ongoing value of the Law (Torah) and the Prophets. The Scriptures of Israel are a repository of fascinating narrative, detailed law, glorious poetry, and prophecy that speaks with heartrending concern for the poor and the exploited, stories of slavery and exile, stories of freedom and redemption. The more familiarity we have with these earlier texts, the more we can appreciate the Sermon's numerous allusions to them.

From those extensions of the Beatitudes, we glimpse one way of reading the Torah. Look to the intention of the commandments, suggests Jesus; build a fence around the Law, and around your own life. When you are tempted to do what is not good for you, build fences to help you resist this temptation. Although the Bible should not be reduced to a self-help book, it anticipates many books that do help us live better lives. We can more carefully check our anger, refocus our desires, and be careful about what we promise. I find particularly compelling Jesus's teachings on reconciliation: don't offer your sacrifice if you have something against another—or, in modern terms, don't wait to be asked to pass the peace in order to create that peace. We cannot be fully reconciled to the divine if we are not reconciled to each other.

Those extensions also give us permission to interpret Scripture since interpretation of those earlier texts did not stop with Jesus. Paul, Peter, James, and on through to the priest or pastor who delivered the sermon last week are all interpreters of Scripture. Jesus, like the rabbis of the Mishnah and Talmud, knew that changing times required changed understandings. They all debated what to take literally and what to take metaphorically, what was appropriate for all times and places and what was appropriate in just one place and one time.

The Our Father, still recited by countless individuals and countless churches, needs to be savored and studied. Each phrase, almost each word, scintillates with meaning.

Where next, now that you're on the path? One way to keep the trail from getting choked with weeds is to continue reading in Matthew. In the introduction, we discussed how Matthew artistically and compellingly anticipates chapters 5–7 by planting references to it throughout the first four chapters. Now, start with Matthew 8, appropriately a group of healing narratives, to show how the Sermon plays out. The stories stand well on their own, but when they are heard as a continuation of the Sermon, they show how the teachings play out in real life—Jesus's and ours.

Another approach is to inventory our lives, as the Sermon hints when it speaks about the narrow gate, the log in the eye, and the impossibility of serving God and mammon. When we declutter, we are better able to focus. At the same time, we have to be careful lest we risk becoming neurotic about following the Sermon. One of its goals is to help us find peace. It is not designed to make us feel despair or guilt or shame; to the contrary, it leads us to the kingdom, to repair, to wholeness.

I wish I could say with Jesus, "Don't be angry," and, "Don't worry." I wish I could stop feeling anger, and I wish I could stop worrying. To enter into the kingdom, we not only read back to the Scriptures of Israel and back to Matthew's first four chapters, and we not only read what comes next in Matthew's Gospel. We read forward into the New Testament. Here's one example of how reading the rest of the New Testament in light of the Sermon works. Ephesians 4:26 reads, "Be angry but do not sin; do not let the sun go down on your anger." When we put this verse in the context of the extension—"But I say to you that if you are angry with a brother or sister, you will be liable to judgment; and if you insult a brother or sister, you will be liable to the council; and if you say, 'You fool,' you will be liable to the hell of fire" (Matthew 5:22)—we understand both verses better. Jesus is forbidding the anger related to murder and so to sin. Ephesians makes clear that other forms of anger—anger at poverty, anger at disease, even anger at the divine for the way we perceive we have been treated on earth—are permissible, for they are not sins. More, Ephesians advises that if we are angry, we do not allow it to consume us. By bedtime, let it go.

Please savor the Sermon on the Mount. Read the rest of the Scriptures through its teachings, and let the texts inform one another. Then share your readings with your friends, and your enemies. If you let the Sermon be your guide, you will not only have one foot in the kingdom of heaven but also be able to experience that kingdom in your life and in your heart.

NOTES

1. The Beatitudes

1. Amy-Jill Levine and Ben Witherington III, *The Gospel of Luke*, New Cambridge Bible Commentary (Cambridge: Cambridge University Press, 2018).
2. Jim White and Robert Dilday, "Campolo Asks Baptists, 'Which Jesus Should We Preach?'" Baptist Standard, January 30, 2008, www.baptiststandard.com/archives/2008 -archives/campolo-asks-baptists-which-jesus-should-we -preach/.
3. "Rashi on Genesis 7:4," Sefaria, www.sefaria.org/Rashi_on_ Genesis.7.4?lang=bi.
4. Dio Cassius, *Roman History, Volume VIII: Books 61-70*, trans. Earnest Cary and Herbert B. Foster, Loeb Classical Library 176 (Cambridge, MA: Harvard University Press, 1925).

2. The Extensions

1. Ulrich Luz, *Matthew 1–7: A Commentary*, Hermeneia (Minneapolis: Fortress, 2007), 226.
2. This Mishnah quotation is taken from Sefaria.org, www .sefaria.org/Mishnah_Makkot.1?lang=bi.
3. See the discussion in Amy-Jill Levine and Marc Zvi Brettler, *The Bible With and Without Jesus: How Jews and Christians Read the Same Stories Differently* (New York: HarperOne, 2020), forthcoming.
4. Flavius Josephus, *The Antiquities of the Jews* (4.280), trans. William Whiston, Lexundria, https://lexundria.com/j_aj /4.280/wst.
5. Charles Duke Yonge, trans., *The Works of Philo Judaeus: The Special Laws* (London: H. G. Bohn, 1854–1890), 3:183.

6. Joseph Stein, *Fiddler on the Roof* (1964), act I, prologue, www
   .bournplayers.org.uk/Fiddler/doc/script.pdf.
7. Art Swift, "Americans: 'Eye for an Eye' Top Reason for Death
   Penalty," Gallup, October 23, 2014, https://news.gallup.com
   /poll/178799/americans-eye-eye-top-reason-death-penalty
   .aspx.

3. Practicing Piety

1. Josephus, *Antiquities of the Jews* (18.12), https://lexundria
   .com/j_aj/18.12/wst.
2. Josephus, *Wars of the Jews* (2.166), https://lexundria.com
   /go?q=J.%20BJ%202.166&v=wst.

4. Our Father

1. Fredrick J. Long, "Roman Imperial Rule Under the
   Authority of Jupiter-Zeus: Political-Religious Contexts and
   the Interpretation of 'the Ruler of the Authority of the Air'
   in Ephesians 2:2," in *The Language of the New Testament:
   Context, History, and Development*, ed. Stanley E. Porter and
   Andrew W. Pitts, Linguistic Biblical Studies (Boston: Brill,
   2013), 133.
2. "The Lord's Prayer (alternative)," *A New Zealand Prayer Book,
   He Karakia Mihinare o Aotearoa* (Auckland, NZ: Anglican
   Church in Aotearoa, 1988), 181.
3. See Amy-Jill Levine, *Short Stories by Jesus: The Enigmatic
   Parables of a Controversial Rabbi* (New York: HarperCollins,
   2014).

5. Finding Your Treasure

1. Originally from Cicero's *Orator*, found in *Oxford Dictionary
   of Phrase and Fable*, New Edition (Oxford: Oxford University
   Press, 2005), 243.
2. Maturin M. Ballou, *Treasury of Thought Forming an
   Encyclopedia of Quotations from Ancient and Modern Authors*
   (Boston: Houghton Mifflin, 1894), 162.

6. Living into the Kingdom

1. See Amy-Jill Levine, *Short Stories by Jesus: The Enigmatic
   Parables of a Controversial Rabbi* (New York: HarperCollins,
   2014), 148.

Notes

2. *Machzor Rosh Hashanah Ashkenaz*, "Musaf, Second Day of Rosh Hashana, Kedushah," Sefaria.org, www.sefaria.org /Machzor_Rosh_Hashanah_Ashkenaz%2C_Musaf%2C _Second_Day_of_Rosh_Hashana%2C_Kedushah?lang=bi.